Stock Market for

GN00733793

Walking on the Masters' shoulders: The Authoritative Guide on How to Invest Like WARREN BUFFET and Others Big Investors. Buy and Sell in Stocks Like a Pro

1

Disclaimer

This Book is provided with the sole purpose of providing relevant information on a specific topic for which every reasonable effort has been made to ensure that it is both accurate and reasonable. Nevertheless, all information herein is for informational purposes only, not intended for trading purposes or advice, and does not constitute recommendations or endorsements of any issuer, security, or action.

While some of the information herein is from sources believed to be reliable, the author does not warrant their completeness and accuracy and should not be relied upon as such when making your investment decisions.

Besides, the author doesn`t make any guarantee as to any results that may be obtained from its content.

No reader should make any investment decision without first consulting his or her financial advisor and research and due diligence. Neither the author nor any of his associates are liable for any informational errors or opinions contained in this book.

This is a legally binding declaration that is considered both valid and fair by both the Committee of Publishers Association and the American Bar Association and should be considered as legally binding within the United States.

The reproduction, transmission, and duplication of any of the content found herein, including any specific or extended information will be done as an illegal act regardless of the end form the information ultimately takes. This includes copied versions of the work physical, digital, and audio unless the express consent of the Publisher is provided beforehand. Any additional rights reserved.

Furthermore, the information that can be found within the pages described forthwith shall be considered both accurate and truthful when it comes to the recounting of facts. As such, any use, correct or incorrect, of the provided information will render the Publisher free of responsibility as to the actions taken outside of their direct purview. Regardless, there are zero scenarios where the original author or the Publisher can be deemed liable in any fashion for any damages or hardships that may result from any of the information discussed herein.

Additionally, the information in the following pages is intended only for informational purposes and should thus be thought of as universal. As befitting its nature, it is presented without assurance regarding its prolonged validity or interim quality. Trademarks that are mentioned are done without written consent and can in no way be considered an endorsement from the trademark holder.

Table of Contents

Introduction

If you are reading this book it's because, like me a few years ago, you are looking for legal and effective ways to maximize your capital and start taking your life to the next level. Regardless of your financial situation right now, for a moment I would like you to consider a metaphor regarding capital accumulation.

Think for instance, when a couple is in the process of having their first child. Usually, while waiting for the big day to arrive, both parents start budgeting and anticipating all the things that they will need in order to accommodate all the needs of the new baby, how much they will cost and what impact the entire situation will have on their expenses and lifestyle. Well, this is exactly your position right now while thinking on how to approach this new business adventure. You are trying to think of all the possible costs and trying to anticipate all the possible consequences on your finances and lifestyle. And, quite rightly so! In fact, this is the best thing you can possibly be doing right now. And the good news is that, if you start looking at your new financial adventure as if you were about to have a child you can actually plan precisely how much you will need and assess exactly what is coming to your way. This method of accumulation can be applied even if you do not have children to raise, but with a view to retirement or if you want to create a general Capital Accumulation Plan (PAC).

Without too much diversion from what we are actually interested in, let's look to the following table regarding exactly how much it costs to support a child from birth onward in a developed country. Let us consider an average $100 a month you would obviously spend $1200 in a year for each child. Now, if instead of raising a child you invested your $100 a month following the strategies contained in this book, you could maximize your investment exponentially. It only takes a clear Capital Accumulation Plan (PAC). Let's look at the example below:

Assume running a PAC up to 19 years of investment.	
Initial investment	$0
Annual interest rate	12,00%
N° annual installments	12
Single installment investment	$100

	Years		
	1	$1.344,00	$2.544
	2	$2.849,28	$4.049
	3	$4.535,19	$5.735
	4	$6.423,42	$7.623
	5	$8.538,23	$9.738
	6	$10.906,81	$12.107
	7	$13.559,63	$14.760
	8	$16.530,79	$17.731
	9	$19.858,48	$21.058
	10	$23.585,50	$24.785
	11	$27.759,76	$28.960
	12	$32.434,93	$33.635
	13	$37.671,12	$38.871
	14	$43.535,66	$44.736
	15	$50.103,94	$51.304
	16	$57.460,41	$58.660
	17	$65.699,66	$66.900
	18	$74.927,62	$76.128
stop PAC	19	$85.262,93	$85.263

6

20	$95.494,48	$95.494
21	$106.953,82	$106.954
22	$119.788,28	$119.788
23	$134.162,87	$134.163
24	$150.262,42	$150.262
25	$168.293,91	$168.294
26	$188.489,18	$188.489
27	$211.107,88	$211.108
28	$236.440,82	$236.441
29	$264.813,72	$264.814
30	$296.591,37	$296.591
31	$332.182,33	$332.182
32	$372.044,21	$372.044
33	$416.689,52	$416.690
34	$466.692,26	$466.692
35	$522.695,33	$522.695
36	$585.418,77	$585.419
37	$655.669,02	$655.669
38	$734.349,31	$734.349
39	$822.471,22	$822.471
40	$921.167,77	$921.168
41	$1.031.707,90	$1.031.708
42	$1.155.512,85	$1.155.513
43	$1.294.174,39	$1.294.174
44	$1.449.475,32	$1.449.475
45	$1.623.412,36	$1.623.412
46	$1.818.221,84	$1.818.222
47	$2.036.408,46	$2.036.408
48	$2.280.777,47	$2.280.777
49	$2.554.470,77	$2.554.471
50	$2.861.007,26	$2.861.007
51	$3.204.328,13	$3.204.328
52	$3.588.847,51	$3.588.848
53	$4.019.509,21	$4.019.509
54	$4.501.850,32	$4.501.850
55	$5.042.072,36	$5.042.072
56	$5.647.121,04	$5.647.121
57	$6.324.775,56	$6.324.776
58	$7.083.748,63	$7.083.749
59	$7.933.798,47	$7.933.798
60	$8.885.854,28	$8.885.854

In the above example you can see a 12% annual profit from your ETFs (Exchange-Traded Fund). Imagine now how much money goes through your hands every month, and through the years, without you even realizing it. You can now start envisioning how to make an accumulation plan straightaway, and if you are lucky, with an even larger sum every month. In this book you will find numerous ways on how to invest this money in the most profitable global ETFs (Exchange-Traded Fund) and other financial tools to maximize your capital accumulation even if you have never traded before. The stock market is the greatest opportunity machine ever created. Are you ready to get your piece of it?

The fundamentals of the stock market

The right investment attitude, essentially, is a blend of six key characteristics. Over time, it is the right investing approach that will have the impact between an acceptable auditor and a dependably productive financial expert.

What do we understand by the expression "Investing Mindset?" Essentially, it is about the mental and intellectual nature of the financial expert. Remember, investing is as a lot of a mental intermingling as it is a series of skill and data. To be sure, even with the best of abilities and all-around data, you are most likely not going to win as a fiscal expert if you don't have the right investing viewpoint. The right risk perspective, essentially, is a blend of six key characteristics. Over time, it is the right investing attitude that will have the greatest impact upon developing the skills of a good financial expert and a consistently productive auditor.

1. Mental balance is the key

What do we fathom by mental prudence? It is the ability to think indisputably despite when markets are unusual, and the financial expert is under tremendous weight. Usually, this is when most financial expert will as a rule sway and accept veritable contributing failures. Believe it or not, mental aptitude is about the calm that you can keep up despite when the market appears to go against you. There are two extreme perspectives to mental balance. Stock exchanges are driven by fear and insatiability.

9

Ordinarily, financial experts will get energetic at the most elevated point of the market and terrible at the bottom of the market.

2. Not just peace of mind, but also balance

Definitely balance is uniquely connected to peace of mind. Balance is like feeling a rock independently of what is going on. For example, self-restraining is the opposite of being greedy in any business sectors at any time. However, you need to act or restrain from acting in some circumstances. So if you get this mix wrong, if you are out of balance, you could create for yourself major misfortunes. The balanced point between this two extremes is where you want to be when you take decisions. The point of these basic principles are: avoid choosing major endeavor when you are in a state of ire or dissatisfaction; And similarly, avoid investment decisions when you are in a state of uneasiness or doubt; And above all, keep away from taking authentic venture decisions in a state of vitality, since you are well on the way to overstretch yourself.

3. Do whatever it takes not to seek after returns, seek after the right framework.

If you are more focused on the results rather than the technique, if you are more worried over the closures than about the strategies, then you have an attitude to problem with respect to investing. Remember, investing is substantially more of getting the framework right. How you recognize stocks, how you screen stocks, what are the non-cash related parameters you consider, how might you impact on the channel and the boundaries of security, how might you incorporate a motivation by aligning your passage and leave levels; all these are bits of your methodology or system. Your considerations should be on fulfilling this methodology and the results will follow naturally.

4. Be a self-motivated student and act with determination

The stock exchange is a remarkable teacher, yet, to really take in the fundamental activities from the market, you should be an excited observer and a self-motivated student. The best way to deal with gain from the market is to listen energetically to what the market is trying to tell you. Endeavor to record the learning's from the market consistently and it can transform into your Bible for exchanging. The embodiment of the issue is that your viewpoint should be that of a self-student. The market isn't the place you will be demonstrated the nuances. It is a monstrous gathering of data from which you can liberally draw upon.

5. Be humble to recognize challenges and your mistakes

If you don't practice calmness in your practices, then investing isn't for you. The best of financial experts gets their assumptions wrong. Attempt to be humble enough to concede that you weren't right and make appropriate helpful change (s). If pride drives you to either average the position or outflank the market, by then you will have a certifiable attitude problem when you are investing. Recognize that the market has a lot to demonstrate to you and recognize your mistakes. That is the route into the right investing attitude.

6. An ounce of movement justifies a pound of orchestrating

You can make the best of plans within the planning stage before trading. There are a couple of things about the stock exchanges that you can adjust just once you start exchanging with real money. Amusement can simply take you so far! Grasp a frame of mind that is action planned rather than delighting a great deal in craftiness. Finally, that is what makes a difference!

The 4 Different Money Mindsets of Investing

1) People Who Prefer to Give Their Investing Capital to Someone Else

These individuals are deliberately missing out on investing in light of the fact that they recognize that they are occupied with different things that are otherwise important to them.

In this manner, they give their cash to a common investment manager and take essential money management plan from somebody who gets you a 3% return on your cash. You surely aren't getting the advantages you merit by having another person deal with your cash and you completely don't have the foggiest idea of where your money is invested.

2) People Who Don't Want to Learn to Invest

They don't recognize they can do it; these individuals are purposefully careless about investing in light of the way that they trust it's difficult to learn or not worth the work.

The marvelous thing about following up on profits is that it continues working when you aren't. You need to invest some work directly, yet over time you essentially find the opportunity to watch your cash make in profits.

3) People Who Have No Money (Or Think They Don't Have Enough Money)

These people think they need money to be an analyst and are coincidentally doing nothing to participate in the process of investing money. You can make sense of how to invest without a tremendous measure of money. I've clarified the most ideal approach is to save $500 to begin investing.

The cash related trade recommends the group of business segments and trades where regular exercises of purchasing, selling, and issuance occur, to detained bits of openly held companies. Such financial activities are exchanged with customary trades or over the counter (OTC) business centers which work under a depicted plan of principles. There can be unmistakable stock trading locales in a nation or a country, which permit trades stocks and different sorts of stock.

While the two terms - insurances trade and stock trade - are utilized at the same time, on the other hand, the latter term is commonly a subset of the first. If one says that she trades the financial trade, it derives that she purchases and sells shares/values on (in any occasion one) of the stock trade(s) that are a part of the general insurances trade. The essential stock trades: the U.S. combine the New York Stock Exchange (NYSE),

Nasdaq, the Better Alternative Trading System (BATS); additionally, the Chicago Board Options Exchange (CBOE). These driving national trades, near to a few different trades working the nation, structure the cash related trade of the U.S.

Regardless of how it is known as a cash related trade or financial element and is basically known for trading stocks/values, other financial affirmations - like Exchange Traded Funds (ETF), corporate securities and reinforcements dependent on stocks, commodities, financial structures, and insurances - are additionally exchanged the investments trades.

Understanding the Stock Market

While today it is conceivable to buy about everything on the web, there is consistently an entrusted market for everything. For example, individuals drive to city borders and farmlands to buy Christmas trees, visit the nearby timber market to purchase wood and other essential material for home merchandise and revamps, and go shopping in Walmart for their standard basic sustenance commodities supplies.

Such committed markets fill in as a stage where various purchasers and merchants meet, group up, and execute. Since there a lot of people selling goods, one is guaranteed of a reasonable cost. For instance, if there is just a single seller of Christmas trees in the whole city, he will have the chance to charge any amount he feels satisfied with, and the purchasers won't have any place else to go. Perhaps the number of tree dealers is great in a standard business center; they fight with one another to draw in purchasers. The purchasers will be overwhelmed to make decision with low-or limited faultless regarding making it a reasonable market in relation to openness. Without a doubt, even while shopping on the web, purchasers' separate costs offered by various brokers on a practically identical shopping path or transversely over various ways to get the best arrangements, persuading the particular online sellers to offer the best cost.

A cash related trade is an equal given market for trading different sorts of confirmations in a controlled, secure, and known environment. Since trading in investments have reasonable surveying practices and openness in trades, an enormous number people who wish to purchase and sell shares have joined the market. While prior securities trades used to issue and plan paper-based physical deal confirmations, the moved to PCs helped cash related trades that today work completely electronically.

How the Stock Market Works

Practically, insurances trades give a protected and composed condition where market people can execute in shares and other qualified financial instruments with sureness with zero-to low-operational risk. Working under the depicted guidelines as imparted by the controller, the financial trades known as crucial markets and as optional markets.

As an essential market, the investments trade enables relationship to issue and offer their plans to the standard open, through the procedure of Initial Public Offerings (IPO). This movement engages relationship to raise noteworthy capital from experts. In a general sense, it gathers that an affiliation disengages itself into various shares (state, 20 million shares) and sells a touch of those shares (state, 5 million shares) to customary open at a value (state, $10 per share).

To support this method, a company needs a business model where these shares can be sold. This business model is given by the stock exchange. If everything goes as per the plans, the company will successfully sell the 5 million shares at a cost of $10 per offer and accumulate $50 million financial profits. Financial experts will get the company shares which they can plan to hold for their favored length, completely anticipating rising in share cost and any potential compensation as benefit portions. The stock exchange goes about as a facilitator for this capital raising methodology and gets a charge for its organizations from the company and its cash related accessories.

Finishing the primary run offer issuance IPO exercise called the posting methodology. The stock exchange also fills in as the exchanging stage that energizes standard obtaining and selling of the recorded shares. This contains the secondary market. The stock exchange wins a cost for each exchange that occurs on its establishment during the discretionary market activity.

The stock exchange bears the commitment of ensuring respected openness, liquidity, regard divulgence and rational transactions in such exchanging activities. As for all intents and purposes, every noteworthy security exchange over the globe work electronically, the exchange keeps up exchanging systems that beneficially manage the buy and sell orders from various market individuals. They play out the financial planning ability to empower exchange execution that is financially sound for the buyers and vendors alike.

A documented company may similarly offer new, additional shares through various commitments at a later time, as through rights issue or through sought after profit on shares. They may even repurchase or delist their shares. The stock exchange empowers such exchanges.

The stock exchange normally makes and keeps up various market-level and part unequivocal pointers, like the S&P 500 record or Nasdaq 100 document, which gives a way to pursue the improvement of the general market.

The stock exchange, moreover, keep up all company news, presentations, and financial disclosures, which can be typically received to on their official destinations. A stock exchange also supports diverse other corporate level, exchange related activities. For instance, beneficial companies may compensate investors by paying profits which usually begins from a bit of the company's salary. The exchange keeps up every single such datum and may reinforce its plan to a certain point.

Components of a Stock Market

A stock exchange fundamentally serves the following with limits such as:

Sensible Dealing in Securities Transactions: Depending on the standards of premium and supply, the stock exchange needs to ensure that all captivated market individuals have minute access to data for all buy and sell masterminds, also helping in the sensible and direct evaluating of investments. Besides, it should moreover perform gainful organizing of appropriate buy and sell orders.

For example, there may be three buyers who have put orders for acquiring Microsoft shares at $100, $105 and $110, and there may be four vendors who are glad to sell Microsoft shares at $110, $112, $115, and $120. The exchange (through their PC performed robotized exchanging systems) needs to ensure that the best buy and best sell are composed, which for this circumstance is at $110 for the given rate of exchange.

Powerful Price Discovery: Stock markets need to help a gainful segment for value revelation, which implies the display of selecting the right cost of a security and is ordinarily performed by assessing business sector free market action and various components related with the exchanges.

Express, a US-based programming affiliation is trading to a detriment of $100 and has a market capitalization of $5 billion. A news event comes in that the EU controller has compelled a fine of $2 billion on the company which on a very basic level recommends that 40 percent of the affiliation's finances might be retrieved. While the financial trade may have obliged a trading regard degree of $90 and $110 on the affiliation's offer worth, it ought to proficiently change the reasonable trading regard

18

most outrageous to suit the potential changes in the offer cost, elsewhere investors may battle to trade at a reasonable cost.

Liquidity Maintenance: While getting the measure of purchasers and sellers for a specific cash related security are foolish for the financial trade, it needs to guarantee that whosoever is qualified and prepared to trade gets moment access to placed orders which ought to get executed at the reasonable cost.

Security and Validity of Transactions: While more people are essential for proficient working of a market, an identical market needs to guarantee that all people are checked and are unsurprising with the crucial norms and guidelines, blocking by default any of the social events. Likewise, it ought to guarantee that each and every related substance working in the market should in like way cling to the benchmarks, and work inside the legitimate structure given by the controller.

All Eligible Types of Participants Strengthen: A business center is made by an assortment of people, which publicize creators, fiscal experts, dealers, researchers, and hedgers. These people work in the investments trade with various businesses and points of confinement. For example, a financial expert may purchase stocks and hold them for total agreement spreading over different years, while a shipper may enter and leave a situation within seconds. A market producer gives principal liquidity in the market, while a hedger may get a kick out of the chance to trade subordinates for coordinating the danger related with investments. The financial trade ought to guarantee that every single such part can work

19

well, satisfying their ideal occupations to guarantee, the market keeps working valuably.

Investor Protection: Along with rich and institutional financial authorities, an incredibly colossal number of minimal financial pros are furthermore served by the stock exchange for their constrained amount of risks. These investors may have limited financial data and may not be totally aware of the snares of placing assets into stocks and other recorded instruments.

Why you Invest in Stock?

Let me cut straight to the chase. Regardless of whether you're a conservative investor that is soon going to go into retirement or you're a young person just out of high school or college, you need to know why you need to invest. This is really important because a lot of people think that stock investing is just another option out there besides saving.

Well, they are two totally different things. A lot of people are under the mistaken assumption that as long as they save money from their income and set aside a certain percentage religiously, month after month, year after year, decade after decade, they will be fine. I'm sorry to disappoint you, but that is not a winning strategy.

In fact, you are playing the game to lose if you are just going to rely on your savings. Why? There is this thing called inflation. Put in the simplest terms possible, inflation is an economic effect where the amount of goods and services one dollar buys this year is going to be worth less next year and the year after that, and so on and so forth. Ultimately, you reach a point where your dollar is no longer able to buy much of anything.

If you think this is crazy or far-fetched, you only need to realize that back in the 1800's, a full-time salary for somebody was a few dollars per month. Obviously, people can't live on that now. That just goes to show you the power of inflation because a dollar back in 1860 is worth so much more now in terms of today's dollar's purchasing power. That's how bad inflation can be.

Even if you looked at as recently as 10 years ago, the food that you could have bought back then, you can no longer buy now. For example, if you walk into a Taco Bell and spend money on a burrito, that money that you spent 10 years ago, is probably not going to buy the same number of burritos today.

Inflation is a serious problem and simply saving money is not going to fix it. You have to find a way to grow your money. This is why stocks are so hot. Stock investing enables you to beat inflation.

If inflation is going up at a rate of 2-5% a year, you can rest on the fact that, if you put your money in a general stock fund that tracks the market index, your money may grow 10-15% per year. In other words, you beat inflation by as much as 13% or as little as 5%. Whatever the case may be, you're still beating inflation. Your money is not losing its value.

Historically speaking, stocks have appreciated in the range of between 12% to over 15% per year. That is amazing inflation protection. While real estate can give you better returns on average, real estate also can suffer a reversal.

If you don't believe me, look at the average real estate values in the United States as a whole after the great financial crash of 2008. You'd be surprised as to how quickly million-dollar homes went down in value.

While real estate, generally speaking, offers a great amount of inflation protection, you would be better off with stock investing.

- "To Everything There Is a Season "

Why is it so essential to measure a company's growth relative to the same duration a year previously? Due to the fact that lots of businesses see their earnings fluctuate in patterns within the year. If you simply compare the most recent quarter to the one 3 months back, you might screw up your growth analysis.

Many natural-gas utilities make good revenue in the December and March quarters, but routinely lose cash in the June and September quarters when the weather condition is warmer, and few clients warm their homes. Additionally, most retailers create more powerful sales during the vacation season than they provide for the rest of the year. Per-share earnings earned by the department shop chain Macy's highlight this seasonality.

Companies often leave out things from their revenues. For example, a producing company might leave out the cash it invested to settle the gain, or a suit is made by offering a factory. You might hear these exclusions called unusual items, unique products, or excellent products. The experts who follow the company most likely do the exact same (and so must you) if the business says it excludes these items from its incomes. A lot of companies that omit items from their profits will provide the adjusted revenue number in a table. However, some businesses will make you do the computations. If all this seems like work, you heard right. Keep in mind, if investing were easy, everyone would do it, and everyone would develop confidence in their stock analysis. Don't worry, the task isn't as tough as it sounds-- and the real mathematics is easy.

As long as you've got the release of the income in front of you, grab the quarterly sales numbers too. Do not stress, you will not need to exclude anything from sales.

Calculating running capital needs some additional steps. For something, not all companies present a statement of money flows in their profit's releases. You'll have to dig a slightly deeper and inspect out if yours doesn't SEC filings. Practically every business will either supply the filings by themselves site or offer links to a third-party website that stores them.

In other words, if a company generates $100 million in operating money flow in the first quarter and $80 million in the second quarter, the second-quarter statement of cash flows will note an operating cash flow of $180 million-- the sum of the first two quarters. Unless you start with the money flow for the first quarter of a business's fiscal year, you'll require deducting the worth from the past quarter's statement to acquire a real quarterly number.

Now that you have enough data to compute the most current quarter's development, next up is tracking 12-month development. Essentially, repeat the preceding steps-- find quarterly profits, sales, cash flow, and prior-year earnings data-- until you've collected four quarters worth of data for each figure. Add the quarterly numbers, and you have all you require to calculate tracking 12-month development.

Now gather the data needed for determining four-year annualized growth. While calculating four-year development needs you to go even further back, yearly data requires a lot less work to acquire.

To gather per-share profits data, download business earnings releases for the fourth quarter of the last and for the 4th quarter of the four years previously. If the company's past fiscal year ended in 2012, you'll require annual data from financial 2008. Discover the numbers that exclude all the special products, and then tape those revenues.

Sales and cash flow are even much easier. Since it provides five years of annual information, which neither Yahoo!

Start with the earnings statement. Choose the alternative for yearly data and grab the sales numbers. After you've obtained your sales data, move to the cash-flow declaration for operating money flow. Now you've gathered all you require for the historic development rates.

Lastly, you can find everything you need for the estimated current-year, approximated next-year, and approximated five-year annualized development rates in one spot.

Visit the analyst price quote page for your stock at Yahoo! Financing or MSN Money and select the following numbers:

The per-share-profit estimate for the present. Approximated per-share profits for the next financial year. Per-share revenues for the last fiscal year. Growth rate for the next 5 years.

After you have actually gathered all of these numbers, stop for a minute and pat yourself on the back. Finish doing your research study on a couple of stocks, and you will not be a beginner for long.

Determining Growth Rates

Now all that stays is mathematics. Before you start, examine the data for three possible problems.

Negative numbers:

You require two stats to compute development rates-- the most recent period and the historic duration-- and your estimation won't suggest anything if either of those numbers is negative. You may still be able to draw some conclusions, though. If a business moves from unfavorable revenues or money circulation to positive, that's great news-- your stock has actually gone from a loss to again. If a company moves from negative incomes or capital to a smaller sized loss (to put it simply, from-- $1.00 per share to--$ 0.50 per share), that's typically great news too-- your stock has narrowed its loss. Naturally, if the loss expands or the stock goes from earnings to a loss, the news has gotten even worse.

Blanks:

Maybe you selected a business that hasn't been around enough time to supply all the needed historical information points. Some companies don't have profit estimates, and if you opted for a utility or a financial business, you might not have any cash-flow data. Don't try to insert the data you do have into a customized result if you can't find any of the numbers needed for a specific estimation. Simply forget computing that development rate.

Magnitude. Did you get all the numbers? If your numbers show a company generating sales of $520 million last year and $48 million the year before, you may want to confirm and make certain you didn't include an absolutely no to last year's sales or leave a number off the past year's.

Often sales truly will leap 983%, however not really often. If you suggested tape-recording $480 million (rather of $48 million) for year-ago sales, the development rate falls to 9.8%, a far more affordable number for the majority of business.

Information about the Stock Market

Let us know peer into what the stock market is. At its basest form, owning a stock is not much more than owning a piece of company where the stock originated from. You become a holder of equity when you buy into a stock. This generically means that you will do well if the prospects of the company do well. Similarly, if the company takes a downturn, then your stock value will then probably depreciate.

Many folks find this easy to grasp, while others still think that the stock market is just a screen or a website which shows ticking jumping numbers. Behind those ticking jumping numbers are actual companies present in everyday life. This gives us an insight to one of the ways of investing in the stock market. You will realize or discover many things if you just stop and ponder a little deeper for a bit. Everyone loves to have the example of Apple stock, but maybe a lesser known name like Keurig Dr Pepper may draw a bit of your attention. This stock is what most investment folks' term as a consumer staple stock. When you break down that $50 dollar word, consumer means folks like you and I, while staple means you really can't do without it for any extended period of time. Things like foodstuff, drinks, as well cleaning items will come into mind when we talk about this. Key to this is also the fact that staples tend to get purchased consistently. If you love doughnuts, and Krispy Kreme is one of your top choices, you just might have known about Keurig if you thought about it and dug a little deeper.

What I am getting at is this. There are many stocks out there, as there are many investment opportunities. Not all of these money-making stocks are known only to the top analysts and hot shot investors. Many have household brands in their stables and we just have to dig a little deeper into the things we use, the things we like, and we just might be able to find a potential winner.

Beyond knowing that a stock is essentially a piece of a company, we have also got to know some of the technical bits. The stock counter or the ticker is the representation of the company in the stock market. Whenever you want to buy or sell a stock, that is one of the most crucial things you need to inform your broker.

Dividends

Companies want as many people as possible to buy their stock. For this reason, many offers what is called a *dividend*. A dividend is a payment companies issue to shareholders each quarter, which equates to a percentage of the share price. This percentage is known as the dividend yield.

For example, AT&T (T) currently sells for around $38 a share. Their dividend yield is currently set at 5.41%. This means that annually, you will earn 5.41% in profits on top of wherever the stock price moves. So, if you were to buy $10,000 worth of AT&T stock, and the price stayed at $10,000 for the entire year, you would receive $541 worth of dividends, split out each quarter. This comes out to about $135 a quarter.

Dividends are issued quarterly, when companies announce earnings. To earn this dividend, you must own a stock before it declares its ex-dividend date, which is usually about 2 weeks before the company actually pays out its dividend. You may be thinking why not just hold a stock for two weeks, sell it, and rake in the dividend? Unfortunately, this is all calculated into the price. What happens is on the day a dividend is paid, the stock price moves down by the same amount of the dividend payment. So ultimately you need to hold the stock for the long term to get the most benefit from dividends.

There are many companies which have increased their dividend payment every year for 25+ years straight. Knowing this, and because dividends tend to pay at a higher rate than savings accounts or government bonds, many traders of retirement age own dividend stocks. They then live off the dividend payments through their retirement years. For example, $1,000,000 is the typical amount many financial advisors suggest clients to have saved by the time they retire. If a retired individual owns a dividend stock which has a 4% dividend yield, they are receiving $40,000 a year in dividend checks. Considering most bills are paid off by retirement age (house, car, etc.), this provides plenty of income to live off of while keeping their primary capital intact. And of course, many dividend stocks rise in price over the years. This means not only are dividend checks being received, but the capital is also increasing.

Charts

There are a number of places to perform research on stocks, as in places where you can look at charts and financial information to see how a stock is performing. Two free websites beneficial for this are Yahoo Finance and FinViz.

Chart Type

There are three main charts used by various traders when viewing stocks. They include the line chart, the bar chart, and the candlestick chart. Here is an example of the stock Snapchat (SNAP) shown on a line chart.

Here is the same stock shown on an open, high, low, close (OHLC) bar chart, and then shown on a candlestick chart.

For most traders, the line chart is fine to use for everyday analysis. One disadvantage to it however is it only shows the closing price, which is displayed in the form of a line throughout the chart.

The OHLC bar chart and candlestick chart show additional information. They not only show the closing price, but also show the opening price, low, and high of a given time period (5 minutes, daily, etc.). Whether a trader decides to use a line chart, bar chart, or candlestick chart is personal preference. I prefer to use candlestick charts when I am researching stocks.

And just to clarify, when you are looking at a "daily" chart, you are not looking at just one day's worth of a stock price. The whole chart shows a specified date range you set, while each individual candlestick in the chart shows one day's worth of trading.

If you were instead looking at a "15 minute" chart, each candlestick would be showing 15 minutes' worth of trading. A 5-minute chart, each candlestick would show 5 minutes' worth of trading, etc. The whole chart itself shows the date range you specify. If this is confusing at all, it will make more sense once you look through a few charts.

Chart Scale

Along with the type of chart used, charts also have two scales: logarithmic and linear. The linear scale is the most common, and what is shown on almost every broker or website you visit. It displays the same amount of space between all price numbers.

For example, the chart below is a linear scale chart of AMD. You'll notice that the spacing between $10-$20 is the same as between $20-$30. However, thinking about this with a math brain, you may recognize that from $10-$20, the stock has actually increased 100%, while from $20-$30, the stock has only increased 50%. So, the range shown is not actually proportional to the percentage the stock increased, but instead just equally spaced between dollar amounts.

The logarithmic scale chart is different because it takes the percent change into account, as opposed to just the dollar range. The same stock is shown below, except this time in a logarithmic scale. As you can see, it takes into account percentage change, and spaces the dollar amounts out proportionally. Thus, it ends up showing a different looking version of the same chart.

Which scale type a trader chooses to use is a personal preference.

Volume

As briefly mentioned before, volume is synonymous with the number of trades, both buying and selling, that take place in a given time period. Generally, when there is more volume, there tends to be a smaller bid/ask spread.

Volume is usually shown at the bottom of charts, in the form of lines. I have an example below with a chart of Coca-Cola (KO).

The chart shown is a "daily chart," meaning each volume bar at the bottom of the chart represents one day's worth of trading volume. So, from Dec. 2019 - Feb. 2020, between 3 million - 20 million shares of KO were bought and sold on any given day.

There are a number of different times frames you can look at charts, which include 5-minute, 15 minutes, daily, weekly, etc. The volume shown directly correlates to whichever time frame chart you are viewing. For example, if you were viewing a 5-minute chart, each volume bar at the bottom would include 5 minutes' worth of trading volume.

For the most part, especially if trading well-known companies, you don't have to worry too much about volume. It becomes more important when dealing with thinly traded stocks (e.g. penny stocks), and certain trading strategies in which volume can be used as an indicator.

Stocks, ETFs, and Mutual Funds

While you're already familiar with what a stock is, you may not know what ETFs and mutual funds are.

Mutual funds were the first on the block, being offered to retail investors in 1974 by Wells Fargo. Many financial advisors suggest "diversifying" a portfolio in order to achieve beneficial returns, while also limiting risk. This would mean instead of just putting all your money into one stock, you would split your money into multiple stocks. This way if one ends up not doing well, you have a number of others which will likely be okay.

Unfortunately, this was hard for everyday retail investors. Not only would you have to keep up with the top companies in the market, you would also need to pay commission on each trade. And remember, commission during this time was very expensive. Mutual funds alleviated all this, as they allowed investors to buy an already diversified set of stocks consolidated into one ticker symbol, which was actively managed by a mutual fund manager for a small fee.

For example, a popular mutual fund created by the company Vanguard is the Vanguard 500 Index Fund (VFINX). This mutual fund correlates to the S&P 500, meaning a consumer could buy this mutual fund with their broker, and essentially own all the S&P 500 for a one-time commission fee. The disadvantages to mutual funds are the limited hours of the day you can trade them, as well as the fees taken by the mutual fund company to balance the fund for you.

In the early 1990s, the first exchange traded fund (ETF) was introduced. Similar to mutual funds, they allowed traders to diversify their portfolio by buying just one symbol. ETFs gained more popularity than mutual funds though because they could be bought and sold like a stock during normal trading hours, and the fees associated with owning them were much lower.

Today there are hundreds of ETFs available for traders to buy, in sectors such as the S&P 500, gold, oil, retail, and any other category you can think of. Within the last 20 years, 2x and 3x leveraged ETFs have also become available, which essentially double or triple your purchasing power when you buy them.

For example, a popular ETF which correlates to the S&P 500 has the ticker SPY. If you were to buy $10,000 worth of SPY, and the S&P 500 went up 1%, your account would also go up 1% ($100). A popular 3x leveraged ETF that correlates with the S&P 500 goes by the ticker symbol UPRO. If you had instead invested this same $10,000 in UPRO, your account would be up 3% ($300).

Of course, this also works in reverse. Meaning if the S&P 500 went down 1%, your account would now be down 3%. So, the leveraged ETFs essentially become a gamble. The stock market is Wall Street's casino!

While items like contango and backwardation can affect the prices of leveraged ETFs, just know they are essentially doubling or tripling your risk/reward when you buy them. These terms are beyond the scope of this book, but you're welcome to look them up if you choose.

Earnings

Each quarter, publicly listed stocks are required to report their *earnings* to investors. While the exact date a company reports their earnings vary, most companies report them around the same time as each other each quarter.

Earnings are a very important metric for companies, as it lets investors know how the company is performing, and if they are making sufficient profits. Before earnings announcements, financial analysts who work in banks and other large corporations predict the earnings per share price they expect the company to announce. Generally, how it works is if a company beats estimates, the stock price will rise, while if they miss the estimates, the stock price falls. This is not always the case however, as other factors may skew the stock price.

Stocks can experience huge gains or losses on days they announce earnings, in the double-digit percentages. Generally, it's not a good idea make short term "bets" on earnings, as it's essentially playing the roulette wheel at a casino, and betting on black or red. Also, many times the analysts are wrong, and sometimes wrong big time. Don't ever rely on analysts! I would compare them to palm readers, as they do not know what is going on behind the scenes and are making "educated guesses" for their estimates.

Splits

Companies like to keep their shares below a certain price in order to attract more investors. So, when a company's stock price gets too high, many will declare a *split*. A common example is a 2:1 split, which is when the number of shares outstanding double, and the stock price splits in half. So, let's say you owned 10 shares of Apple at $200 each, which equates to $2,000. Apple declares they will be performing a 2:1 stock split. You now own 20 shares of Apple at $100 each, again totaling $2,000. Meaning your account value doesn't change, just the number of shares you own and the price of the stock.

Splits usually indicate a company is doing well, as their stock price has moved high enough for the company to be able to partake in a split.

The opposite of this is called a *reverse-split*. This is where a company's stock price has moved too low, and in an effort to make their stock price look more attractive, they perform a reverse-split. A common example is a 1:10 reverse split. For example, let's say you own 100 shares of ticker symbol CRAP, currently trading for $0.50 a share ($50). The company declares a 1:10 reverse split. You now own 10 shares of CRAP, valued at $5.00 a share ($50).

Reverse-splits generally indicate a company is doing poorly, and 95% of companies that declare a reverse split never come back to their pre-split price. Exchanges such as the NYSE and NASDAQ delist stocks which move below $1. Considering a company never wants to be delisted from an exchange, this is another reason they would perform a reverse-split.

How the master's Tell us to Invest in Stock Market (Warren Buffet)

Simply put, Warren Buffett did not become perhaps the greatest investor in all of history by being a short-term thinker. Neither did he become one of the industry's most quoted men by holding his tongue and keeping his opinions under a cloak. Warren Buffett's easy-to-understand advice, folksy way of imparting it and utter humility in answering questions once they are asked all combine to make him one of the finest men out there to take advice from. We will start the journey of learning from Warren Buffet by looking at some amazing investing lessons that will make a great difference as you invest.

- The Art of Stock-Picking

"If you are not willing to throw away the misplaced romanticism in stocks and put in the time and work that stock-picking demands, then the guy on the opposite side of your trades will likely know more than you do"

Here is where we start when it comes to Warren Buffett and his advice on going for stock: it is not a hobby and thus, should not be treated as one. It is important to understand that picking stocks is not like picking up groceries at the store. Here is what Warren Buffett admitted to doing: when he was starting out, he reckons he spent thousands of hours learning about the stock world and the means of maneuvering; today, he reckons he has doubled that tally. Learning the skills required to build substantial investment is vital, as is taking the whole thing seriously.

Warren Buffett used to camp at his local library until he had read every investment publication the library could offer. When he was through with them, he re-read them again, and then some more. If that sounds nondescript to you, then you should know the man was only 11 at this time.

The bottom-line is this: if you are not willing to throw away the misplaced romanticism in stocks and put in the time and work that stock-picking demands, then the guy on the opposite side of your trades will likely know more than you do. This often translates to the ultimate underperformance recipe.

- Leave Emotion at The Door When It Comes to Investing

"Emotion only guides you to refusing to admit missteps and mistakes; to hold onto a losing project for far too long rather than simply cut your losses, put your business trench coat on and move forwards."

Mike Tyson once said that it was in his nature, just as it is in every human being in the world, to be given to emotion and act based on it. If anything, life is so much the wealthier for it. However, the glamour of emotion, unfortunately, does not extend to the investment world.

Emotion greatly eats away at investment returns. If you truly are keen at making some costly systematic mistakes, have emotion as your sidekick as you invest. Emotion will likely also bring its close cousins, cognitive bias and ego, along for the ride too, very much at your expense. Here is what emotion makes you do: rather than dig deep and look for evidence that may fight your position (and thus perhaps save you a lot of misery in the future), it wires you to look for only that evidence that supports it. You will only start to seriously ponder about risk when things are already heading south. Now, while this is bad enough in most areas of life, it has the capacity to be very destructive in the investment world.

Emotion only guides you to refusing to admit missteps and mistakes; to hold onto a losing project for far too long rather than simply cut your losses, put your business trench coat on and move forwards.

Emotion is a funny beast in how it works too; rather than have a clear head of what you expect to make and reinvest, it focuses you too much on how you will spend the money you earn from the investment you are making. Is there anything wrong with this? Not necessarily, until you come across Warren Buffett's wise words. He said, "You do not spend the money you get from investments, you reinvest it again".

Besides, the overconfidence and excessive optimism that emotion pins to your belief of your investment abilities is far too dangerous in the investment world. Keep emotion off your workstation.

- "Invest in Familiarity"

If there is one thing that Mr. Buffett stressed on over and over again is the importance of having a flat circle of ultra-competence. Basically, what this points to is investing in an industry that is clearly marked out, a business model that has been carefully drawn out, an investment style that has a sheaf of factual material to back it up etc. Of course, you must continue to learn, thereby making the circle larger. Warren Buffett has 3 mailboxes he keeps on his desk. The labels on them are "in", "out" and "too difficult". Every business has, admittedly, factors that qualify as known, unknown, vital and unimportant. For maximum gains though, Buffett recommends that you invest in a business in which the vital/important factors are known. Why so? According to him, the only reason he will pick something is to be with it for the long haul. He wants to estimate, with a degree of accuracy, how that business will look like in 5 to 10 years.

So, what does this mean to you as an investor? Always invest in investments that you are familiar with or at least industries that you know a thing or two about. However, this does not mean that you simply stick to such businesses or investments. Your goal is to continue learning and improve your knowledge of different kinds of investments therefore, increasing your chances of succeeding in any kind of investment you make.

- Owning Stock Is Owning A Business, Not A Bunch of Digital Charts

"You need to think of it (owning stock) as something of a partial ownership in the main business body that underlies it"

You cannot afford to look at stock as an over-glorified line on a chart that moves up, at least hopefully, over time. You need to think of it as something of a partial ownership in the main business body that underlies it. Unlike, say, precious stones or collectibles, stocks have intrinsic value attached to them because your very ownership gives you a claim of proportion to the corporation's earnings in the future. How so?

44

In the form of dividends, of course. If the business does well in a stretch of time, the price of the stock will eventually follow suit. Warren Buffett looks at himself, not as an analyst of the market or perhaps an analyst of the macroeconomic sort, but as an analyst of business. It is time you viewed yourself as so.

- Don't Gamble with Your Money

Many people think that investing in the stock market is a lot like gambling, but in fact the two activities are very different. Warren Buffett has spoken out about gambling in the past, which he has called an "ignorance tax" because it preys on the stupid. He even likens speculation, which he has spoken out against in the past, as being like gambling.

The main difference between gambling and investing is that your success in gambling is almost entirely dependent on chance, and there is basically nothing you can do to influence the outcome. Investing, on the other hand, involves studying the asset to determine whether or not it is worth buying. While luck can affect the outcome of your investment, its influence is very minimal. If you have done your homework, it is almost certain that you will see a return on your investment.

As an investor, you should understand and accept that stock picking involves a lot of hard work. You cannot just leave your stock picks up to chance and hope that you will enjoy a return. You have to take the time to study the fundamentals of the asset carefully to see if it is worth your money. If you are not willing to do this, then you are effectively gambling with your money.

- Reinvest Your Profits

Warren Buffett's road to building wealth is a testimony to the effectiveness of this lesson. When he was in high school, he and a friend placed a used pinball machine, which they had bought for $25, in a local barbershop. The machine proved to be popular with the barbershop's clientele, such that they were soon reaping handsome profits.

Instead of spending their money on frivolous things, as you would expect high school students to do, they instead reinvested their profits and bought more used pinball machines. In time they had eight machines in shops all over the area. Eventually they sold the machines, and Mr. Buffett reinvested in profits in stock. By constantly reinvesting his profits, he had earned $174,000 by the time he was 26, or $1.4 million in today's dollars.

It's not only your profits from investments that you can reinvest. If you have an unexpected windfall, such as a bonus from work or a tax refund, you can reinvest most or even all of it. By doing this, you can put your money to work earning more returns.

- Be Different

When it comes to investment, one of the most important lessons you can learn is being able to form your own opinions. Mr. Buffett has said that listening to the market opinions of others is a "waste of time". What is important is that you are able to perform your own analysis and make your own determination as to whether or not an asset is a worthwhile investment.

Another lesson worth reiterating is that you have to learn to go against the herd. One of the reasons why stocks experience price volatility in the short-term is because they are always being affected the views of market participants about them at any particular time.

For example, if a company issues an earnings report and it does not live up to analysts' expectations, you can expect its price to dip. On the other hand, if there is news that it is about to release a new product in the market, its price will go up. But these price changes don't really reflect what the fundamentals of a company are. As a value investor, it is up to you to research these fundamentals so that you can determine if the company is a good long-term investment.

Don't focus on price action; otherwise you'll be a speculator. Or as Mr. Buffett puts it: "Half of the people who bet on a coin toss will win their very first bet, but none of them will see a profit if they continue playing."

- Limit Your Borrowings
Warren Buffett has repeatedly made his feelings clear about the use of leverage, or borrowed money, to invest. He has been quoted as saying that he has seen more people fail because of leverage, adding that you really don't need a lot of it. "If you're smart," according to Mr. Buffett, "you'll be able to make a lot of money without leverage."

One of the worst things that you can do as an investor is to borrow money to finance your investments. Unless you are assured that your investment will generate enough cash flow to cover your debt repayments, you should not do it. This is particularly true for value investors, since you are holding your stocks long-term and not selling them to generate a quick profit that you can use to repay your debt.

Instead of borrowing, grow your holdings gradually. Buy a small amount of stock and then add to it when you can afford to. If your stocks generate returns in the form of dividends, reinvest the dividends in more shares of stock. If you absolutely must borrow, then make sure that you limit the amount to the absolute minimum that you need and repay it as quickly as possible.

- Assess Your Risks

One of the reasons why Warren Buffett has been so successful as an investor is his ability to assess and manage risk. While a certain amount of risk is inherent in any investment, the wise investor chooses the asset whose risks fall within what he is comfortable accepting.

But just what is risk? There is a simple definition, according to Mr. Buffett – risk is simply the probability that you will lose your investment. The higher the probability, the bigger the risk. If the risk is too high, Mr. Buffett simply does not invest in the asset.

One way that Mr. Buffett assesses risk is by looking at the potential rewards and seeing if the risk he is accepting is worth it. As he puts it, if you buy a dollar for sixty cents, it is riskier than if you bought it for only forty cents. However, in the latter case the expectation for reward is greater; the higher the potential reward, the less risk there is.

Thus, once again, it boils down to doing the hard work and carefully studying any investment before you jump into it. Or, as Mr. Buffett puts it – Risk is when you don't know what you're doing.

- Know When to Walk Away

Although Warren Buffett is an advocate of holding stocks long-term, he does not hesitate to unload a stock when it makes sense for him to do so. For instance, Berkshire Hathaway used to be one of the largest shareholders of Exxon Mobile. Mr. Buffett has said that he believes Exxon to be an outstanding company. At the time he bought his stake, however, oil prices were at a high, and his partner Charlie Munger expressed the opinion that oil would become very high priced as supplies tightened. Unfortunately, crude oil prices started falling and as a result, Mr. Buffett unloaded Exxon Mobile at the fourth quarter of 2014.

The lesson to learn here is that you should not hesitate to respond to changing market conditions. If you feel that the initial reasons why you made the investment are no longer valid, you should not hesitate to get out of it.

Additionally, you should not hesitate to adjust the size of your holdings when it suits your investment goals. For example, Mr. Buffett reduced his stake in Wal Mart and Goldman Sachs, not necessarily because he thought there was something wrong with these companies, but because he needed to free up money to acquire Precision Castparts. You can follow Mr. Buffett's example by reducing your exposure to some stocks if you feel the money can be better invested elsewhere.

- Understand the True Meaning of Success

One of the most important lessons that Warren Buffett can teach investors is that they should not measure their success by the amount of money they accumulated, but instead by the personal satisfaction they enjoy in their lives. When he was asked about how he personally defines success, he quoted the old saying about how success is when you get what you want while happiness is when you want what you get. He said in this case, he prefers happiness to success.

Another important point to consider when measuring success is not to use external measures. Mr. Buffett has said that it is important for you to consider your "inner scorecard" – how you personally feel about success – rather than how the rest of the world perceives whether or not you are successful.

And one last takeaway: true success means that you should always strive to be a good person, according to Mr. Buffett.

ETFs: What are they and how do they work?

ETFs: what are they?

ETFs (Exchange Traded Funds) are regulated financial instruments and not OTC (like forex) as they are traded on a regulated market, such as the Italian stock exchange.

Why do you need to know what ETFs are and how they work, especially if you are new to financial investments?

I believe that ETFs are in fact a "new" investment opportunity that until just a few years ago were closed to individual investors.

ETFs allow the investor to:

achieve greater autonomy and independence from the banking system;

greater awareness in the choice of their investments.

So what are ETFs?

ETFs are a simple financial instrument, both in their operation and use: for these reasons they can be used by any private investor who wants to invest their savings independently.

Think of an ETF as a fund dressed as an action ... in what sense?

I'll explain right away.

An ETF is like a fund because it replicates the set of shares of a fund just like a mutual fund (the ETF, however, is passively managed while the fund is actively managed).

Both the fund and the ETF allow you to diversify on the market with one click because you do not have to manually select the securities, but with one click you buy the instrument and you have an already diversified investment.

However, I anticipate that there are important differences between mutual funds and ETFs, including significantly lower costs in ETFs. I explored the topic in the article "Differences between ETFs and funds: find out how much you can save every year".

You can consider the ETF as a stock at the same time because you buy and sell it immediately as if it were a stock, at the current market price.

Therefore, from a practical point of view, buying an ETF is absolutely identical to buying a stock, but what changes is what is inside an ETF, that is its vast composition.

To give you a culinary example, the action is the single flavor of a tub of ice cream, the ETF is the tub of ice cream, which can contain many flavors inside.

ETFs: how do they work and why is it worth investing in ETFs?

They are a passively managed tool.

ETFs are structured with the aim of replicating the return of a reference index (called "benchmark") as accurately as possible and not offering a higher return than the benchmark itself.

This objective is achieved simply by holding the same shares that are part of the reference index.

Buying an ETF such as the **SPDR S & P500 ETF (Isin code IE00B6YX5C33**), is equivalent to buying with a single click a basket identical to that of the American S&P 500 index, which is made up of 500 US companies with the largest capitalization.

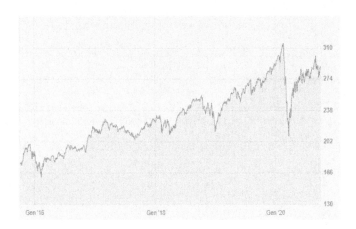

So the performance of your ETF follows that of the replicated index, precisely the American S & P500 index.

Mutual funds, on the other hand, are actively managed financial instruments, that is, there is a real manager who pays because it should make you get a higher return than the reference index.

Unfortunately in 90% of cases (to be broad and optimistic) this does not happen, but you continue to pay high costs every year ... so I advise you to start asking yourself questions in case you have money invested in funds.

Advantages of ETFs

I now summarize the main advantages of ETFs:

1. Diversification: ETFs allow you to invest in many underlings and types of instruments (shares, bonds, commodities, etc.), they allow you to diversify also by income distribution policy ("Distribution ETF" or "Accumulation ETF") ;

2. Liquidity: ETFs are very liquid instruments in general;

3. Transparency: ETFs are listed in real time, so the purchase and / or sale price is transparent at all times; you can also check their returns at any time;

4. Flexibility: ETFs are suitable for any type of investor, from the father of a family to the professional trader; they are suitable for intraday, short-term and long-term operations; allow you to trade long, short and leveraged.

5. Volatility: ETFs have significant internal diversification, which reduces their risk and volatility;

6. No risk of bankruptcy: ETFs have any default risk because they have separate assets from the issuing companies. So even in the event of the insolvency of the latter, your money invested in ETFs remains safe in any case;

7. Low costs: ETFs have no entry, exit and performance commission costs, but the overall cost is reduced to the annual management cost (formerly "TER") and sales commissions;

8. Investment strategies: ETFs allow you to use different investment strategies, namely:

55

- Do trading operations;

- Carry out investing operations - such as the P.I.C. ("Capital Investment Plan") and the P.A.C ("Capital Accumulation Plan") -;

- invest for retirement;

- accumulate capital for your children or grandchildren;

9. Investment even with little money: ETFs do not require a minimum purchase lot, so you can diversify your portfolio even if you have a modest capital; you can also start investing in a PAC with 100 euros / month and take advantage of compound interest;

10. Construction of low cost portfolios: ETFs allow you to create a very well diversified portfolio of stocks, bonds, commodities, etc. with just a few tools, all at very low costs.

At this point the question is legitimate: are ETFs the panacea for all ills?

No, ETFs also have drawbacks.

Disadvantages of ETFs

Here are the few disadvantages of ETFs, which however do not always occur but based on the type of ETF you invest in:

1. Sometimes significant bid / ask spread;

2. The average value traded each day can be low and therefore there may be scarce liquidity;

3. Inefficient taxation;

4. The presence of the Market Maker may be required to ensure liquidity.

So you have read in this chapter how much ETFs are and how they work, their advantages and disadvantages, why it is convenient to invest in ETFs, especially if:

- you want to learn how to manage your savings independently and consciously;
- you want to start investing at low risk,
- you have a modest initial capital to invest,
- you want to accumulate capital over time for your children or grandchildren
- you want to create a pension fund.

Megatrends ETFs

ETFs also allow you to invest in Megatrends, or in those sectors destined to revolutionize our lives.

Megatrends are a very interesting topic for investors today.

What are megatrends?

These are those sectors destined to revolutionize our lives, such as the advent of the internet in the 2000s, for example. In short, they are those overwhelming issues that will transform the economic fabric on a global level.

It would certainly be ideal, for your investments, to dedicate a part of your capital to invest in the megatrends of the future.

What will be the megatrends on which to bet among all the possible ones?

In my opinion, these five megatrends are particularly interesting topics to evaluate for your investments:

- cyber security megatrend;
- megatrend of robotics and automation;
- megatrend of artificial intelligence;
- megatrends on videogames and those games that take place on a virtual level;
- megratend on global health services.

Based on what did I make this assessment?

As always based on the graphs and numbers.

Which ETFs to choose to invest in megatrends?

Now I am going to give you in detail, by way of example and not as an investment advice, the five ETFs you have seen in the previous charts.

ETF "L&G Cyber Security UCITS ETF", ticker ISPY, ISIN IE00BYPLS672, annual costs 0.75%: this ETF invests in companies actively engaged in the provision of IT security services and technologies;

ETF "L&G ROBO Global Robotics and Automation USCITS ETF", ticker ROBO, ISIN IE00BMW3QX54, annual costs 0.80%: this ETF invests in companies around the world related to the robotics and automation sector;

ETF "WisdomTree Artificial Intelligence UCITS ETF", ticker WTAI, ISIN IE00BDVPNG13, annual costs 0.40%: this ETF invests in artificial intelligence companies;

ETF "VanEck Vectors Video Gaming and eSports UCITS ETF", ticker ESPO, ISIN IE00BYWQWR46, annual costs 0.55%: this ETF invests in companies globally that generate at least half of their revenues from video games, e-sports or software or related hardware;

ETF "iShares Healthcare Innovation UCITS ETF", ticker HEAL, ISIN IE00BYZK4776, annual costs 0.40%: this ETF invests in companies from around the world that are engaged in innovation in the field of global health services in developed and emerging markets.

Coronavirus: health and economic crisis

During this stock market crisis due to the Coronavirus, both in the event that you are already exposed with financial investments in place or in the event that you have liquidity to invest and are wondering how to earn with the Coronavirus.

Let's start with the fact that unlike the latest market crises, the Coronavirus is primarily a health and economic crisis, which puts a strain on the economy of over 45 countries worldwide to date.

Coronavirus and the Stock Markets

As with any crisis, the question that is impossible to answer is:

"how long will the Coronavirus last?".

It is obvious that no one can give an exact answer but the only thing we can do, to advance hypotheses, is to look at the statistics and numbers of what has already happened in China.

Consequently, no one knows for sure if this rapid fall in the stock exchanges has settled, I personally think it plausible that the markets can go down a little more, or that the financial crisis due to the Coronavirus can still persist. In fact, remember that economics and finance do not always go hand in hand, quite the contrary.

The speed of descent of the major world indices has triggered the so-called "panic selling", ie a massive large-scale sale of various financial instruments.

You will have noticed that in this specific case everything has collapsed in recent days, including gold, which has always been considered a safe haven par excellence.

Why?

Because the losses on the stock (and bond) market were so high that even large investors (such as mutual fund managers) had to close their gold positions in profit to reduce the aforementioned losses. However, you could probably see gold pick up in the coming months.

How to invest with the Coronavirus?

This is another question that you will have asked yourself if you have money to invest in this period in which Coronavirus and Stock Exchanges are linked.

On the web you will be able to read many and of all colors ... my humble opinion is that this crisis can last a few months or a few more years.

After the Covid-19 virus pandemic, I assume that the stock market will resume an uptrend.

How do I assume it? Once again I rely on the history of the markets and the numbers.

How Long Does is Take to Breakeven?

Peak	Trough	Drawdown	Months	Years
9/7/1929	6/1/1932	-86.2%	159	13.3
9/7/1932	2/27/1933	-40.6%	3	0.3
7/18/1933	10/21/1933	-29.8%	22	1.8
2/6/1934	3/14/1935	-31.8%	6	0.5
3/6/1937	3/31/1938	-54.5%	77	6.4
11/9/1938	4/8/1939	-26.2%	46	3.8
10/25/1939	6/10/1940	-31.9%	32	2.7
11/9/1940	4/28/1942	-34.5%	10	0.8
5/29/1946	10/9/1946	-26.6%	36	3.0
6/15/1948	6/13/1949	-20.6%	6	0.5
7/15/1957	10/22/1957	-20.7%	10	0.8
12/12/1961	6/26/1962	-28.0%	11	0.9
2/9/1966	10/7/1966	-22.2%	6	0.5
11/29/1968	5/26/1970	-36.1%	20	1.7
1/11/1973	10/3/1974	-48.2%	46	3.8
9/21/1976	3/6/1978	-19.4%	13	1.1
11/28/1980	8/12/1982	-27.1%	3	0.3
8/25/1987	12/4/1987	-33.5%	17	1.4
7/16/1990	10/11/1990	-19.9%	4	0.3
7/17/1998	8/31/1998	-19.3%	3	0.2
3/24/2000	10/9/2002	-49.1%	48	4.0
10/9/2007	3/9/2009	-56.8%	37	3.1
4/29/2011	10/3/2011	-19.4%	4	0.3
9/20/2018	12/24/2018	-19.8%	4	0.3

As you can see in this table by Ben Carlson relating to the American S & P500 index, neglecting the great crisis of 1929, given that the world today presents very different political and economic dynamics, the numbers tell us that the average recovery time from a market bearish is around 18 months.

Several drawdowns (the momentary decline of the market) were even recovered in less than a year.

How to invest in Coronavirus ETFs if you start from scratch

In this case, my strategy is instead to start a monthly accumulation plan, if you do not already have significant capital.

If, on the other hand, you want to invest a capital of at least $7,000-10,000 in ETFs, I would immediately invest about 30% of the capital and then continue with the P.A.C. monthly.

This is just to share with you a potential rough strategy, which you can adapt to your needs.

Which stocks or indices to invest in? Personally, I would invest in the S & P500 index or other US indices, and something also in precious metals with "physical" ETCs.

Compound interest is the eighth wonder of the world

I will try to explain in simple words what compound interest is and how to exploit it to get higher returns on your investments.

Einstein himself defined compound interest as the eighth wonder of the world and asserted that "those who understand it gain while others pay";

It is therefore worth investigating what compound interest is, the difference between simple interest and compound interest, how it works and how to exploit compound interest.

What is interest?

Interest, or simple interest, is a sum you pay for having used a financial service, such as the interest you pay to the bank for a mortgage or any loan stipulated.

As you know, the longer the duration of the loan, the greater the overall interest you pay to the bank, because the latter will take longer to collect the entire amount that has been advanced to you.

What is compound interest and how it works

Let's make a distinction immediately: simple or compound interest?

Simple interest is the one defined above, while compound interest is interest on interest.

We contextualize simple interest and compound interest both in the world of financial investments, which is what interests us specifically.

Simple interest is the return that is paid to you consistently, based on an initial invested capital, which does not increase because you periodically withdraw the earnings.

I'll give you a concrete example.

Invest a sum of $20,000 in an instrument with which you earn 10% per annum, you will find yourself a sum of $22,000 at the end of the year; subsequently withdraw the $2,000 of profit and repeat the same investment with the initial capital always of $20,000.

After 10 years you will find yourself $40,000, or you will have doubled the initial capital.

Compound interest, on the other hand, is based on the continuous reinvestment of the accumulated earnings, without the withdrawal at the end of the year.

Take the same example again but, after earning $2,000 in the first year, invest the total accumulated capital in the second year, i.e. the sum of $22,000 and not $20,000 as in the first example.

The initial invested capital will gradually increase after each year and therefore the annual earnings will increase accordingly.

In this second case, after 10 years you will earn $51,875.

In the image below you can see what happens in the two cases of simple interest and compound interest.

Initial Investment	$20.000
Annual interest rate	10,00%
Investment duration (years)	10

Future value with simple interest: 20.000+(20.000*10%)*10 =	$40.000
Future value with compound interest without P.A.C.: VF=20.000*(1+10/1)^10 =	$51.875
Simple net interest	$20.000
Net compound interest without P.A.C.	$31.875

	Int. Simple	Int. Compound without PAC
Total capital	$40.000	$51.875
Interest only	$20.000	$31.875

Do you understand the importance of compound interest and why do you have to use it to earn over time?

Forget simple interest and from now on worry about making the most of compound interest in your investments.

So how to exploit compound interest?

Compound interest: how to exploit it

Now let's see how to take advantage of compound interest in investments or better still what can be the best investment with compound interest, even if you have a small initial capital such as $1,000

You have surely guessed that the factors determined to exploit it and earn more than with a simple interest are two (we will add a third later):

- the time you have available, or the predetermined duration of your investment;

- your ability to be profitable on average every year, but this is valid in any case, even with simple interest.

Compound Interest Calculation Example:

It is equally intuitive that if you have the opportunity to start with a larger initial capital such as a few tens of thousands of dollars, your gain will be significant right away.

Even 10% of a capital of $50,000 in the first year is equivalent to a gain of $5,000, while 10% of $1,000 involves a gain of only $100, but everyone starts investing according to their own economic situation.

But now comes the fun. Even if you initially invest $1,000, you can gradually increase your capital with a periodic frequency, which you choose based on your ability and saving capacity.

You can therefore take advantage of the power of the so-called P.A.C ("Capital Accumulation Plan") which is a form of medium-long term investment, or investing.

With which financial instrument do you create a P.A.C.?

The best investment in my humble opinion and from personal direct experience are ETFs, on which I have specialized in recent years

So choose your ETF or even create a portfolio of ETFs and plan a tailor-made PAC, specifically programs:

- goal of your investment;
- the duration of the JAP;
- frequency of periodic payment (monthly, quarterly, half-yearly or yearly);
- sum to be paid periodically based on your savings capacity.

You can also start directly with a periodic payment if you do not have an initial sum to invest, in short, the P.A.C. is a versatile investment strategy.

It is also always a good time to start a P.A.C., even better if you are in a bear market phase.

However, a fundamental rule to respect: if you start with a P.A.C. of a duration set by you (for example 10 years), do not worry about things happening in the market in the short term (for example after 2 or 3 years), even if it falls due to some financial crisis.

Here is the example given in the chapter:

Initial Investment	$20.000
Annual Interest Rate	10.00%
Investment duration (years)	10

Future value with simple interest: 20.000+(20.000*10%)*10 =	**$40.000**
Future value with compound interest without P.A.C.: FV=20.000*(1+10/1)^10 =	**$51.875**
Simple net interest	$20.000
Net compound interest without P.A.C.	$31.875

Now assume you run a $ 200 monthly PAC:

Initial Investment	$20.000
Annual interest rate	10,00%
N ° annual installments	12
Single installment investment	$200
Investment duration (years)	10
Total capital invested: 10.000+200*12*10 =	$44.000
Future value with compound interest with P.A.C.	**$93.949,65**
Net compound interest with P.A.C.	$49.950

	Int. Simple	Int. Compound without PAC	Int. Compound with PAC
Total Capital	$40.000	$51.875	$93.949,65
Only Interest	$20.000	$31.875	$49.950

Years		
1	$24.640,00	$27.040
2	$29.744,00	$32.144
3	$35.358,40	$37.758
4	$41.534,24	$43.934
5	$48.327,66	$50.728
6	$55.800,43	$58.200
7	$64.020,47	$66.420
8	$73.062,52	$75.463
9	$83.008,77	$85.409
10	**$93.949,65**	

QR Code

DENSO WAVE INCORPORATED

How to Buy and Sell Stocks

How to choose stocks

Having gone through the importance of fundamental analysis and the common indicators/tools that are used in carrying it out, the next line of action is to understand how to apply these indicators to choose the right stock.

- How to Use Fundamental indicators To Pick, Stock

It is important to survey the fundamental and technical factors as their importance cannot be understated. Once several high-returning covered call trades have been obtained, the investor should start with the fundamentals. It should be noted that those who trade based only upon the return offered and who do not evaluate the fundamentals are not in the game very long. Fundamental analysis, is more detailed than the elements presented here. The goal is to assure we of the stock's worthiness and to look for danger signs. This should serve as added information. The following analytical process can be used for this: if a stock does not cut, you should find it out quickly to waste as little time on it as possible. For this reason, the most important fundamental elements are viewed first.

The Price to Earnings (P/E) Indicator: The P/E ratio is not perfect and reveals to us nothing about the nature of profit, or whether income is growing or taking a downturn. Be that as it may, it regardless fills in as a valuable measurement to look at stocks in a similar industry. A P/E ratio fundamentally higher than the business average outcomes because the market indeed prefers the stock, yet that preference can change abruptly. If market opinion changes negatively towards that stock, you, as a holder of that stock can sell it. Sell off would be more worthwhile if the stock sold for an overvalued price.

Earnings matter a lot in picking a stock. Stocks with no profit, that is, no earning is dependent on an expected forward P/E, which may never emerge. In a rectification or bear showcase, stocks with no income or an unusually high P/E proportion get affected first and remain down the longest. The main allowable particular case is the larger firms. Companies not bringing in cash are not the best places to invest. You should initially know the average P/E ratio for the company you want to invest in. If the business P/E indicator itself is very high, say more than 50; at that point, sooner or later, the company will sell. Watch for news and assessment of the company for early notice.

Earnings growth and Quality: Numerous occasions sway earnings, including one-time, unprecedented events that are unimportant to earnings quality. By quality, we allude to operational profit (and income), not phenomenal occasions, for example, the offer of a division or a one-time discount. What's more, companies that focus more on earnings, usually report their financial outputs to show more earning quality. Now and then, these incomes exhibited here are sometimes misdirecting. Tragically, profit quality is hard to evaluate without a point by point assessment of companies' financial statements. Hence, you may wish to concentrate on earnings development over time and its dependability, since robust earnings growth is a more applicable metric than earning quality.

A quarterly review of earnings growth will significantly act as an indicator of the stability and value of a company. Indeed, even in a failing economy, well-managed companies will most likely do fine and will further blossom in a healthy economy. Such companies attract conservative traders and long-term investors the same. The five-year development rate likewise is useful, since substantial growth over this period combined with quarter-on-quarter development shows quality. For medium and smaller companies, earnings growth is undeniably more significant than for enormous tops, from the stance of covered risk. As an investor, you should try to maintain a strategic distance from stocks with a P/E of more than 60 for secured calls.

73

Earnings per share (EPS) is emphasized in this respect since it relies upon the number of offers exceptional. A stock buyback would blow up EPS without a relating income increment. What's more, giving new offers such as public offerings, mergers, etc. would diminish EPS, yet the money inflow may be very positive.

- Other fundamental indicators

Buy and hold investors incline toward stocks of companies whose Price to sales ratio (P/S) and price to cash (PCF) ratio are not altogether higher than the industry averages. Cash flow accurately quantifies the organization's operational wellbeing. Stock examiners profoundly view these measurements as markers of valuation reasonableness.

The market wherein a company works ought to be taken a glimpse at for its wellbeing, valuation reasonableness (P/E, and other value products) and performance trend (pattern). On the off chance that the business is drifting down, at that point, the stock must be a lot stronger to justify being its value at the market. Some do not accept this to be significant, yet a stock in a stable industry is bound to perform well, taking everything into account, if every necessary condition is met. On the off chance that the business is selling off, the stock value is likely to drop.

- Average day by day Volume

Although this is more a technical analysis tool but is also very relevant in this discussion. Volume is, by and large, a proportion of the stock's liquidity and dependability, however not really of its necessary sufficiency. Low-volume stocks can give high returns; however, they are dependent upon control and can without much of a stretch be moved. There are an excessive number of incredible assets with substantial volume to allow for the trading of the low-volume stocks. Regardless of whether you are searching for progressively unstable stocks for exchanging openings, pick high volume. The average day by day volume is what makes a difference. Note that volume is only one measurement; a low-quality or profoundly unpredictable stock can exchange huge volumes. It is essential to take everything into account; more is better.

- Stock volatility

Volatility reveals to us how unpredictable the stock, take the most recent incident; for example, Tesla has been, how it rose and dropped sharply in the market. Instability might be level when contrasted with past records, and it can also be expanding or diminishing. Then there is implied volatility that demonstrates whether alternative prices are inferring a potential future unpredictability that is lower than, in accordance with or higher than the past records of volatility.

To go about this, inspect the volatility by contrasting the present 30-day instability with the earlier 30-day time frame, to check whether the volatility is increasing. At that point, take a look at the 10-day volatility to check whether there is an ongoing increment. If there is an increase in volatility, it is crucial to check what the forces are. Under 20% instability is low; however, such stocks don't usually offer a lot of premium returns. Remember that the markets frequently show general volatility of under 15%. 20-40% is a medium degree of instability, and over 40% could be viewed as high. Over 80% is high as can be. This based on personal experience, and it has been corroborated by other analysts and investors who have experience in the market. In the end, no one but you can choose what instability level you are eager to go up against, however staying with more prominent companies with reliable records in the twenty to fifty percent volatility range can yield enormous profits for your investment.

Inferred or implied volatility ought to be estimated against the 10-day volatility. If implied volatility is following the lower 30-day unpredictability rather than the higher 10-day instability, at that point, the later volatility primarily isn't being estimated into the choice; the market isn't worried about it because there is no cause for alarm.

Furthermore, stocks probably won't be especially volatile; however, convey a high background of inferred volatility (unpredictability desires, for example, overhanging annuity issues, or such. This is one preferred position of counseling fixed secured call records: by routinely observing what is on the rundowns, it is simpler to triangulate high-returning stocks with their volatility and suggested unpredictability numbers.

Here and there, it is useful to counsel a central positioning of by and substantial quality. There are online platforms that give such a measurement, which is a mix of functional and essential elements. Some of these platforms likewise clarify in detail the purposes behind the positioning. There are comparative rankings accessible from different sources, too.

A final group you should consider are the Insiders (officials, chiefs, and significant investors). They are bound to record reports when they purchase or sell protections of their companies. These reports are broadly held to demonstrate whether the insiders think about their organization's stock a purchase or a short. This view is commenced on chronicled perceptions that insiders will, in general, purchase their organization's stock when the viewpoint is splendid and sell in front of terrible occasions for the organization. This means well since they have a definitive instructive favorable position. Be that as it may, insider exchanges are a troublesome measurement to utilize. In the first place, insiders will sell in general vigorously when the organization arrives at new highs; or old highs, so far as that is concerned.

Many analyses and forces affect when to choose stocks, how to choose them, when to sell, and hold on to your stock. A strong understanding of these factors and their respective fluctuations would help make you an investment guru in no time.

How to Start Trading

We have already spoken extensively about how to invest in the stock market and how this activity can generate very high profits. Precisely because of a large number of profits that can be obtained, many are those who aspire to become stock traders—but how do you learn to invest in the stock market?

The point is that the exchange is not a game—every time someone uses the term "play in the stock market" is taking you on the wrong path, as it is not a game—it is about investment. The best way to learn how to invest in the stock exchange is to start investing with an intuitive and easy-to-use broker. What's the best solution, in my opinion? It's definitely *24option*. Among other things, those who register for free at *24option* also get free excellent trading alerts with which to invest in the stock market is much easier.

- Invest in a Stock from Home

The first characteristic of the investment in the stock market that immediately jumps to the eye is that it is an investment that can be made directly from home. It is no longer necessary to go to the Bank to hand over the purchase orders to the employee on duty. With a little nostalgia, the old traders remember those bank branches that had become a bit of a meeting place for the oxen park, considering the large number of traders who met and exchanged information and observations. On the one hand, it is a positive thing, since investing in the stock market through an Italian bank is the best way to get skinny off of commissions and to lose money, given the inadequacy of the tools offered.

The only positive aspect of these oxen park meetings was the possibility of transmitting the necessary experience to those who were starting to invest in the stock market. Learning to invest in the stock market using the comments and experiences of older people is something that is difficult to do if you work from home. To solve this problem, it is obviously possible to attend discussion forums and try to establish a dialogue with the most experienced users. It is also advisable to always go very carefully on the forums because not all the information there is correct. Add, however, that investing in the stock exchange from home, using tools such as binary options or contracts for difference, is great more convenient than going to a bank branch physically.

What are the best platforms to invest in home exchange? There are a few platforms that are truly reliable and affordable. Among the best platforms to invest in the Stock Exchange, we can report:

- Plus500: safe and reliable; it is a truly professional platform. Plus500 is a difference trading (CFD) trading platform that allows you to invest in thousands of shares listed in all major world markets.

- 24option: a truly safe and reliable binary options broker, perfect for investing in the stock market.

- IQ Option: This is one of the most innovative binary options brokers. It is very safe and reliable. It offers a free unlimited demo account in time and quantities. IQ Option is the only platform for trading on the stock market that allows you to start investing with just 10 dollars.

- Starting Your Investment in the Stock Market

The first step to start investing in the stock market is to know what the stock exchange is. It might seem obvious, but it's not like that—many traders start stock trading without even knowing what it is. The Stock Exchange is the regulated financial market on which shares are exchanged, which represent securities owned by listed companies. Each share gives the right, as the case may be, to receive a dividend (a portion of the company profits that are redistributed) and to participate in the ordinary and extraordinary meetings of a company.

Usually, however, it is not advisable to invest in the stock market through the shares. The best way to start investing in the stock market is to focus on derivative contracts that have underlying shares. In this way, you get the advantage of increasing earnings and, above all, earning both when stocks go down and when they go up, obviously making the right prediction.

- How to Learn to Play in the Stock Market

At this point, you may ask how to learn how to play the stock market? The title of this paragraph is a provocation because we know that we must not talk about gambling but about investing. In any case, how do you start? How do you learn? The best way to start is options. These derivative instruments, in fact, are very simple to use and understand. In fact, binary trading is very easy—if we choose a stock listed on a World Exchange (one of the main ones, of course), we only have to indicate whether the price of the asset will be increased or decreased at the end of a period of time. It does not count the level of variation; only the sign counts. This is perfect for learning because the aspiring trader can concentrate only on a few fundamental factors, leaving out all the details. It must be said that options trading can produce profits so high that many traders are choosing to trade options only, although they do not need a simplified approach.

- How to Operate on the Stock Exchange

We have already seen that in order to operate on the stock exchange, it is convenient to use derivative instruments; binary options are better to start with and, later, CFDs can also be adopted (contracts for difference). Another important choice to make to invest in the Stock Exchange, especially at the beginning, is to focus exclusively on the best stocks, i.e., those of large companies listed on the world's major stock exchanges.

Among other things, the major options brokers and CFDs provide access to all the big stocks but not too small listed companies, perhaps in secondary stock exchanges like the one in Milan. In fact, these titles are usually extremely dangerous, and the novice trader who should choose them would be at serious risk of losing money.

Resources and Strategy

The Importance of Strategy

There is no perfect and ideal technique in trading that applies to all traders and all situations. We can even say that there are as many trading styles as there are traders. The market operator must be wary of the one-size-fits-all solution or miracle system simply because the markets are changing, and what works today will be less effective tomorrow. He must not try to be right, but to maximize his chances of success.

After defining the strategy, we will highlight the main strategies adopted in the business world and we will see to what extent they can be applied to trading.

Strategy Definition

A trading strategy can be defined as the art of detecting the best opportunities offered by the market and allocating the necessary resources to profit from it. It will consist of understanding the psychology of the speakers and developing a method to capitalize on this knowledge. The goal of the strategy is to be original, powerful and offer a real advantage over the competition.

The development of the strategy and its implementation imply for a trader to have a strong trading system and control his emotions. In fact, we realize that the trader is often the victim of his own bias, that he does not have a real system and that even if it is the case, it will systematically deviate.

The strategy is materialized by the strict and rigorous application of a trading plan including tested and tested rules that will allow the trader to capitalize on recurring figures without neglecting the risk. This strategy will make it possible to define:

How it will determine the entry points by taking into account the money management aspect as well as the technical aspect; the different techniques to make profits; the manner in which the stops will be fixed; the contingency plan which specifies the different approaches of the trader in the face of the disaster scenarios.

Strategy and tactics are often confused: the strategy aims at absolute performance, in other words, victory, whereas tactics are a means to achieve it. Strategy plays an important role as it allows the trader to get out of the chaos that reigns in the fight by keeping in mind firmly rooted principles.

Tactics are at the service of strategy and must never take too much liberty with respect to strategy. This principle is the key to victory, but it is often forgotten by traders and explains for a large part the failure of many of them.

The trading plan will, therefore, include different tactics but must also specify the global strategy of the trader that can be called vision. That is to say that the trader must in his trading plan specify how he sees himself in a few years (the vision) and indicate the strategy that will be put in place to achieve it.

The Different Strategies

Several types of strategies make it possible to succeed. The strategy of global dominance by the costs mainly benefits institutional traders who have extremely low transaction costs and can benefit from small market movements. Generally, they work for large institutions and have a real advantage over individuals. Their fixed costs (hardware, software, offices, etc.) are reduced because of their size and the large sums they brew. In addition, they have an important information network that gives them a real advantage over others.

The Differentiation Strategy

For a company, differentiation is about creating a product that offers qualities that justify a higher price and a real advantage over the competition. This is the case of innovative products, quality of service, a more efficient organization of work, etc.

Similarly, the trader has every interest in differentiating himself from his competitors by developing a concrete advantage. He can, for example, find a niche and develop an advantage in it. He can also develop an original method and apply it on a regular basis. It is important to note that in the most important trading is not to find a revolutionary method to predict the evolution of stock prices, but simply to find a method with an interesting probability of success and to apply them on a regular basis. But often, traders will not respect their system and will be victims of their emotions. Differentiation consists in having an irreproachable preparation and developing a solid and efficient system.

The Emerging Strategy

This strategy does not question the two preceding strategies. A trader can opt for global domination by cost or for differentiation and from time to time adopt an emerging strategy.

An emerging strategy can be defined as a strategy that arises from action. A trader can, for example, be bearish on the market and sell short several securities, then realize that the market holds, that it is not really bearish and that some elements point even in the direction of a bull market. The trader realizes that his idea of origin no longer works and his action makes him realize that the markets are bullish. It will be able to be based on this observation and to place itself in the purchase.

To illustrate the concept of emerging strategy we are mentioning the experience of a financial author, from March 2000.

On March 26, 2000, I gave a lecture on the technical indicators at the Technical Analysis show in front of a sold-out room. My diagnosis on the NASDAQ was still bullish and I explained, showing the index graph, that there was currently no danger in this market which remained well oriented with an RSI above 50%. Nevertheless, the main risk was the presence of a bearish divergence not yet validated. If it were to be, we could see a bearish stall.

86

A few days later, Abby Joseph Cohen, chairman of the investment committee of Goldman Sachs explains "that it reduced from 70% to 65% the share of the shares in its standard portfolio, because of the recent rise of the courses". It was not necessarily bearish as it held 65% equities in its typical portfolio, but the sharp drop in markets validated the bearish divergence.

Then, I understood the issue and I realized that the market is really drawing a major reversal. Indeed, the bearish divergence on the NASDAQ was confirmed by other downward divergences validated on the main European stock market indices (CAC 40, Dax 30, etc.). I, therefore, went bearish on March 29, 2000, on the main indices IS & P 500, CAC 40, DAX 30, MIB ...] and I recommended my clients to sell their securities. This was certainly an emerging strategy since I relied on new elements that I did not have."

This example shows how important it is for a trader to be flexible and never stubborn. It's a good trader's job not to have a fixed opinion and to let the market behavior dictate what to do.

When to Sell a Stock

The last step for an investor to claim his gains is to sell his stock. Assuming that the investor followed the previous steps correctly, the investor will almost be guaranteed a large gain. However, the investor needs to decide when to sell the stock in order to maximize his profit. An investor wants to avoid selling a stock too early or too late because it will not allow him to maximize his gains. For long-term investors who look at business fundamentals, there are only a few cases in which they should sell their shares: the business model changes, the business becomes financially unstable, or if the market price is above the fair price.

The first reason to sell one's shares is if the business model changes. The business model is the way the business operates: the customer the firm targets, the way the firm makes money, the products the firm sells. When the firm changes a significant portion of its business model, an investor should consider whether the business is still worthy to invest in because the changes may make it less profitable. For example, in 2014, Amazon was an online store and that is about it. However, in 2017 and 2018, it made significant changes to its business model. The firm added many new services and business segments: Kindle Direct Publishing, Amazon Web Services, Whole Foods, and smart stores. Anyone who owned Amazon's stock before these additions and changes must consider whether the company is still worth owning because the changes could make the firm weaker. For example, when Amazon decided to buy Whole Foods, some investors were concerned that Amazon made a poor decision by investing in physical stores because many people believe that they were dying out. Considering that Whole Foods represents a significant portion of Amazon's expenses, some investors might have sold their shares. Thus, an investor might want to sell his shares of stock if the firm makes significant, adverse changes to the business model.

Investors should also look for adverse business trends when deciding to sell a stock. This means, if a company starts to show signs of failure, the investor should sell his shares because it is likely that the share price will fall along with the business. There are multiple indicators when looking for unfavorable trends.

One of the most important trends to look for is the slow death of an industry. The best example of a company that is experiencing a slow death is Barnes and Noble (BKS)- a major player in the book industry. In the early 2000s, ebook started to become popular among everyday readers. Consequently, readers read less from physical books, leading to less sales for Barnes and Noble. The decline of the physical book industry was paralleled with a decline in Barnes and Noble stock price. On April 1, 2010, the firm's stock price was at $14.46. At this time, some investors realized that ebooks are going to take over, and they sold their shares. However, some did not pay attention to the macro-industry trend, and they decided to hold their shares. Due to their lack of awareness of the industry trends, they had to take major losses. During April of 2019, the stock price was around $5.10; negligent investors lost over 60% of their investment because they did not realize that ebooks were trending. Thus, it is important for investors to look at industry trends.

Investors should also look at financial trends when determining when to sell a business. Unlike when one looks to purchase a stock, investors want to look for declining revenues and profits on the income statement as signals to sell the stock. Investors want to sell the stock if the profits are falling because it could signal the decline of the company. Assuming that an investor purchased his shares in a company while its net income and revenue were increasing, he has most likely made a sufficient return on investment. As long as the company is still growing, the investor should not sell his shares because the value of those shares would most likely rise in value. On the other hand, if the firm starts to see their profits fall, it could signal that the company will start to decline. Then, the investor should sell his or her shares because, over time, the company will become less valuable. The best example of a large firm that started to fail is General Electric (GE), a conglomerate. Throughout 2016, General Electric made about six billion dollars in net income. Although this statistic might make the company seem like a good investment, it was on a downward trend. In 2017, the company lost eight billion dollars and in 2018, it lost twenty billion dollars. If an investor recognized that the firm's profits were declining, he could have avoided large losses; from 2016 to 2018, the stock price collapsed by over 65%. Thus, an investor should look at financial trends in order to look for warning signs when deciding to sell a stock.

The last reason an investor should sell his shares occurs when the market price of a stock is above the stock's fair value. Remember, the fair value of a stock is equal to its future value divided by four. If an investor owns a stock when the market price is above its fair value and continues to hold it, he will not achieve his annual goal of an average 15% gain because the stock price is likely overvalued, which would cause it to fall. Moreover, if the investor owns the stock when it is trading above its fair value, he would have a severe opportunity cost because he could be invested in stocks that are deeply discounted instead of overpriced; by investing in discounted stocks, he would have a larger long-term gain. Thus, an investor should sell his shares if the market price is above its fair value.

If none of the three selling situations- the business is no longer stable, the business model significantly changes, the market price exceeds the fair price- occur, then the intelligent investor should hold his shares because the stock would be trading below its intrinsic value, assuming the investment was not made in a speculative company and the research was thoroughly completed by the intelligent investor. When a stock is trading below its intrinsic value, it is discounted, allowing investors to make a near-guaranteed profit. Therefore, unless one of the conditions occur, the beginner investor should not sell his shares because it will most certainly increase in value because it is trading below its intrinsic value.

Some of the Top Traders in Stock Market

Warren Buffet

When it comes to giving financial advice, few people are able to captivate an audience quite like Warren Buffet can. His extraordinary success in the world of investments - not to mention his $85 billion fortune - means even those not the slightest bit interested in finance sit up and listen when Buffett shares his top tips for amassing wealth.

Yet Buffett is more than just the sum of his bank balance (a ten-figure number to be exact). His life is shrouded in a passion for business and investments and, despite his vast wealth, he is widely known for his generosity and frugality - he still lives in the same home in Omaha in Nebraska that he bought for $31,000 in 1958 and more recently he has pledged to give away 99% of his wealth to charities.

His story is an intriguing one to say the least. Who is Warren Buffet? What are some of his principles that you can apply in your life and business? What can you learn from Buffett's own experiences about managing your life, money and career?

Buffett has already confronted and overcome life's challenges and created a path that could serve as a winning roadmap for you. All you need to do is be willing to follow that path on your way to success. You'll need to tweak and customize it a little to meet your own situations and circumstances, but the blueprint is largely in place. In life and business, you can make the most of the wisdom learned by successful and wealthy people who've made a mark for themselves globally and use it as a guide to achieve your own goals.

For decades, Buffett has been a role model to thousands, if not millions, of budding entrepreneurs and people keen to make a difference in their lives. His success has influenced the actions of business people all around the world and has served as an exceptional standard to strive for both professionally and personally, thanks to his generosity and willingness to help others. His influence spreads far and wide and even those among the richest in the world have adopted Buffett's life approaches. Thanks to Buffett's encouragement, for example, more than 160 billionaires have agreed to donate and give away at least half of their wealth for philanthropic causes.

Paul Tudor Jones

Paul Tudor Jones is an American Investor, a hedge fund manager and he is also known as a philanthropist. Jones was born on September 28th, 1954. His love for Hedge fund management led him to open his firm back in 1980, a company by the name Tudor Investment Corporation. The company's headquarters were and are still based in Greenwich, connect cut, and it specialized in the management of assets. Later on, he created Tudor group which is a hedge Fund Holding Company. The Tudor hedge company specialized in the management of fixed income, currencies, equities and also commodities.

Over the last years, his companies have been doing great earning him great fortunes since in February 2017, he was estimated to have a net of 4.7 billion by Forbes magazine and this made him be number 120 the of the wealthiest people in the world on the category of 400 people ranked on the magazine. Aside from this, Tudor 11 was also named as the 22nd highest and best-earning hedge manager worldwide. Aside from focusing on his hedge business, Tudor has also not been left behind when it comes to the love of humanity. This is traced back to the case where he opened the Robin food foundation just eight years after beginning his hedge firm. This foundation is solely focused on helping to eradicate poverty.

He was born in Memphis, and most of his life was spent there during the school time. This is because he attended the Presbyterian day school and later joined all boys elementary school, and also, he entered the Memphis high school. After graduating from high school, Jones then joined Virginia University, and he graduated with an undergraduate degree in economics in 1976.

He started to work immediately he finished his college education because, in the same year that he graduated, he was able to secure employment at trading floors where he worked as the clerk. He worked there for four years, and in 1980, he was employed as the broker in E.F Hutton and companies. He worked in his new company for about two years before quitting claiming that he got bored by his job. Jones decided to further his education, and he applied at Harvard University in the business school category although he did not attend the school.

Jones Tudor was first helped by his cousin who is the EO of Duvanant Enterprises a firm that is known to be among the top cotton merchants worldwide. William Duvanant introduced Tudor to a commodity broker by the name Eli Tullis who hired Jones in his cotton firm and still mentored him as well. He was trained on the trading and the brokerage work of the New York stock exchange.

According to Jones, Eli was the toughest and the best trainer he has ever come across as he taught him all the traits that one needs to become a successful businessman. He showed him how to withstand high competition in the markets, and he also warned him that whenever you have a business, you will always experience ups and downs in the line of your work.

Tim Cook

Timothy Donald Cook is the American executive, Industrial Engineer, and Developer. He is currently the Chief executive officer at the offices of Apple Inc. This is the new position he acquired at the Apple Inc since he previously worked as the Chief Operating Officer under the founder Steve Jobs. Joined Apple in the year 1998 as the senior vice president of worldwide operations and then he later served as the executive vice president of the world in the department of sales and services. In 24th March 2011, he was promoted to become the Chief executive. He is remembered for his active advocation of various humanity and environmental growth which include the reformation of political of international and local surveillance, cybersecurity, corporation taxation both nationally and internationally. Environments preservation and also the American manufacturing act.

In the year 2014, Cook became public and identified himself as a gay and was listed among the 500 CEO at Fortune magazine. Other companies that Cook worked at include; he was a member of the board of boards of directors of Nike-inc., the national football foundation, the trustee of Duke University.

Around 2012, the Apple Inc company decided to give Cook a compensation of shares worth millions of dollars vesting in 2016 to 2021. During a public speech; Cook said that his earnings from the granted stocks would be offered to charity institutions. This includes all that he owns.

George Soros

George Soros was born in Budapest, Hungary on August 12, 1930 as György Schwartz. He was born to Tivadar and Erzsébet Schwartz. The family was of Jewish descent but chose to not practice their religion due to the fact that anti-Semitism was on the rise in Hungary. As an upper-middle class family, they did not wish to have their family to be under suspect and scrutinized. To avoid this, they changed their last name to Soros, which means "designated successor" in Hungarian. This name was liked by Soros's father not only for its meaning but also because it was spelled the same forward as it is backward.

After this name change, Nazi Germany came to occupy Hungary in March of 1944. The Nazi's established a Jewish Council, Judunrat in which all Jewish children had to report. They were no longer allowed to attended their regular schools. This council was in charge of deporting any Jews that were found in Hungary. They picked school-aged children to be the ones to bring the deportation notices to the people.

At this time, Soros was 13 years old and had received papers himself to give to Jewish lawyers. His father, Tivadar, advised him to warn the people as he handed them out that if they showed up to work that they would be deported.

During this precarious time, falsity needed to be made to protect many of the Jewish people. Soros's parents hid their Jewish roots yet again by purchasing documents that stated their "Christian" faith. This helped them survive through the Nazi occupation. Young George even had to pretend to be the "godson" to an official of the Hungarian government for his own protection. George was put in a situation where he had to go with this official to a Jewish family's estate to take inventory. He was not a part of the process himself, but had to witness the event. The official who was protecting Soros had his close connection to the Jewish people because his wife was Jewish as well. She had already gone into hiding at this point.

Through efforts like these, many Jewish people were protected in Hungary. The efforts of Soros's father to help people during this time solidified in young Soros's mind that his father was a great hero and a protector to the Jewish people.

Finally, an end came to the hiding in 1945 when the Nazi's left their occupation of Hungary. Soros was able to leave Hungary shortly after the Nazi receded in the year of 1947. Now he could pursue an education in London. He emigrated to England where he attended the London School of Economics as a student of Carl Popper, a philosopher. In 1951, he received his Bachelor of Science in Philosophy. He ended school in 1954 with a Master of Science in philosophy.

Carl Icahn

Carl Icahn was born on Feb 16, 1936, and he is a well-known businessman in America. Apart from owning several businesses, he was also and still best known for being a reasonable investor and philanthropists too. He founded the Icahn Enterprises, and he is the controller of all the company's share since he is the largest shareholder. The company is significant, and it is based in the New York City. Lately the company is known as the conglomerate Holding company, but initially, it was referred to as American Real estate Partners. Cahn has also chaired in the Federal-Mogul company which specializes in developing manufacturing and also supplying the powertrain components and vehicle safety products.

Carl has also won hearts of many due to his business tactics whereby he was titled as the corporate raider due to his ability to profit from the hostile takeover and the asset stripping of the American airline. Forbes magazine looked at his wealth, and he is estimated to have a total of 16.6 billion dollars by 2017. He was also ranked as number 26 of the wealthiest people in work on the 400 rich people categories. In the hedge business world, Carl appears to be on top five of wealthiest men taking the last position.

He had also worked with the current American president where he worked as the economic advisor on the financial regulations of the country's before he left due to the conflict that rises in his work.

He grew up at Rockaways Queens part of New York City, and his parents were Jewish. He attended school in the same town. Carl's father was an atheist, a cantor, and also a substitute teacher at the Rockaways schools. On the other hand, his mother was a schoolteacher. After high school, Carl went to Princeton University where he graduated with a degree in Arts in philosophy. In 1957, he also joined the New York University school of medicine, but he dropped out of university to join army reserves after just two years of studying.

Carl secured his first job at the wall streets where he worked as the stockbroker in 1961. Then in 1965, he started his company Icahn CO which was a security firm specializing in risk arbitrage and options trading. Around 1978, he began to focus more on the individual trading companies, and with his excellent work, Carl was able to build up an excellent reputation as the corporate raider most especially after his successful takeover of the Trans World Airlines in the year 1985. He was able to successfully sell his TWA assets as a way of paying back the loan he had taken to start his company. This act was also referred to as asset stripping.

In 1966, Carl acquired the TWA private which made him a profit of about 469 million dollars and in return left the company with a debt of 540 million dollars. In 1991, he sold some of his TWA company shares which were around the American airlines for a total of 445 million dollars. Carl in the same year formed a website referred to aslowestfares.com which focused on selling TWA tickets and in return he acquired portions of the global leisure travel from another company by the name Ramy El-Battani to merge into his TWA company.

In 1986 Carl incurred a vast lost from the launch of his unsuccessful 7 billion hostile takeovers for 89 percent of USA steels company.

In 2001, Carl struck a deal with Riverdale LLC where he sent them a total amount of 100 million, and in return, they were expected to purchase 2 million shares of the company.

In 2004, Carl went to a business battle with Mylan laboratories whereby they both wanted to buy king pharmaceuticals. But Mylan lost to Carl as he offered to pay a considerable amount of money for king something they could not do and he ended up with the company.

Special Interview with Top Trader

Mark Minervini loves to talk stocks. After more than 34 years as a professional trader, he's achieved a reputation as one of the world's best.

Part of his secret has been to stick to a strategy of swing trading growth stocks. In essence, he looks for the biggest moves in some of the market's most exciting and fastest growing companies. But there's much more to it than just reaping big profits from trading in and out of the market.

Mark credits his success to his methodology, discipline and mental strategy. In fact, in his new book, **_Think & Trade Like a Champion_**, he goes deep on the psychological pressures faced by traders and investors, and how to overcome them. His message is that focus and risk management are just as important as good stock picking when it comes to being successful in the stock market.

When I first interviewed Mark back in early 2017, he was just finishing _Think & Trade Like a Champion_. It's a follow-up to _Trade Like a Stock Market Wizard: How to Achieve Super Performance in Stocks in Any Market_, where he sets out his trading strategy in depth. Mark says his new book is essentially volume 2 with much of the material being the information he couldn't fit in his first book.

When we caught up again, we picked up on some of the big trading questions that he covers in his new book and discussed some of the finer points of his strategy.

Mark, right at the end of *Think & Trade Like a Champion*, there's a discussion between you and Jairek Robbins about what you see as the most important features in the mindset of a successful trader. Why do you think the right 'behavior' is so important in trading?

Well, I have a long history of attending workshops run by Jairek's father, Tony Robbins. Jairek himself is like an encyclopedia of mental training techniques, he's really amazing. So, it was an incredible honor and pleasure to work with him at my workshop and collaborating for that chapter in my book.

When it comes to behavior and mental control, the bottom line is that if you think you can't do something, then you are right, you won't be able to. The real key is that humans can only perform up to the level of their self-image or identity. So, the general rule of thumb is, regardless of your skill or ability, you're not going to outperform your self-image.

Whether you're aiming to become an Olympic skier or a stock trader, you're going to have to learn how to perform under pressure. You may do well in practice, but when it comes to performing under pressure you'll only be able to go as far as your level of confidence. If you don't feel that it's "like you" to win, if you don't feel that you can be a great trader, if you don't believe that's your identity, it doesn't matter how much ability you have, you're going to cap-out at your self-image. That's what people ignore, because it's buried in your subconscious and you may not even be aware of it. The key is to build your self-image to a level that is at least equal to your ability. I'm currently writing another book about how to do precisely that and build the mindset of a winner.

Ultimately, I think it's the most important aspect of achievement in any endeavor.

When things are calm and you have time to think, you are operating from your conscious mind. But when the pressure is on and you have to operate very quickly, you revert to your subconscious, or your intuitive mind. Your conscious mind makes decisions slower and can only focus on one thing at a time. But when you let your subconscious mind takeover, you operate intuitively and the self-image is the gas pedal - and that's what guides how well you perform from that point. It's not magic, it's simply the science of how we operate as humans.

What is it about ill-prepared traders that causes them to fail in the market? What do they get wrong and why?

When you're not properly prepared you operate under false representations. People think practice makes perfect, but I know individuals who have been trading for 30 years and they still have miserable results. They just keep doing the same thing over and over. Just doing things over and over won't make you good, in fact, it will make you horrible if you are practicing wrongly. Practice doesn't make perfect, practice makes habitual, so you're just ingraining bad habits. You have to be careful. If you're practicing the wrong things, you're just perfecting mistakes.

The only way practice makes perfect is when you learn to practice correctly; perfect practice. That may require a performance coach if you want to do it quickly. If you want to do it the way I did, you can spend three decades figuring it out - and that's fine too. By the time I worked with performance coaches, I didn't need them. But it took many years of trial and error.

In *Think & Trade Like a Champion*, you cover a lot of new ground around risk management, including subjects like staggered stop losses. Have your views about managing risk changed over the years?

Not at all. Nothing major has changed in the stock market and nothing is going to change meaningfully. Certainly, nothing has changed when it comes to risk. You simply must manage risk because it doesn't manage itself. I always say that trading without a stop loss is like driving a car without brakes. How long do you think you can drive around before crashing?

Staggered stops simply break down a stop into multiple stops at different price levels without risking any more than you would with one stop price. If a stock or the market is volatile, you enter a trade and set an eight percent stop, you can maintain the same level of risk by setting a stop on half the position at six percent and then putting the other half at 10 percent. What will happen is that you'll choke off two percent on the front half but you'll give it two percent more on the back half and maybe give yourself a better chance of staying in a portion of the trade.

It's a trade off, but when there's a situation when the market is volatile or I want to make sure I'm in a 'key leader' - especially at the beginning of a new bull market - I don't want to get knocked out of an important stock. I'd rather have a half position in an important stock than no position at all. So, I'll give it a little more room on half by breaking the stop up. And you can break it up into three or four stops if you want. The important thing is to bracket those stops around the percentage number that you want to end up at, so that it averages the risk you are willing to take.

Another new topic in the book is the question of when stocks should be sold. Why do you think this is such a big challenge for many traders?

Taking a profit is a harder decision than buying because buying is more mechanical and selling is more subjective. You get into all these kinds of emotions around anticipation, regret and worry about where the price is going to go. But the bottom line is that most traders have the wrong idea of what trading is actually about. Speculation is about selling higher than you buy and doing it as many times as you can. You always have to keep your eye on the ball. Most traders get caught up in highs and lows and Monday morning quarterbacking. If you lose focus on what the goal is - to make a decent profit and do it again - then you'll get yourself very frustrated and confused.

Some investors will say: "I should have held because it kept going up. Obviously, I sold it wrong because it went higher."

Or they'll say: "I should have sold because it went down."

That may or may not be correct.

Sometimes you'll make a good decision and lose money and make a bad decision and make money. You should never conduct post analysis and judge something right or wrong necessarily by the result. The result doesn't always justify the means. Just because you took a risky trade and made money, that doesn't mean it was a good decision. You have to go in with a plan and then judge your trade on the quality of the plan and how well you stuck to your plan.

It's a very systematic way of thinking. Do you think there are certain characteristics needed to be successful in trading and investing that only exist in very few?

No. The traits needed to be a stock trader can be learned. No-one is a "natural" speculator at birth. I think anybody could do it. It requires a roadmap, sound principles, discipline and then experience. Oh, and you need to learn how to keep your ego in check.

It doesn't matter whether you want to become a basketball player, an Olympic athlete, attorney, doctor or a stock trader. The reason only a few reach the top in any of these fields is not because of special talent or pedigree, it's because most people simply don't believe they can perform at a high level. Like I said before, you can only perform up to the level of your self-image. It's the confidence in your own ability that's really important.

Most people spend their time and effort trying to learn how someone like myself trades, when in fact they should be trying to learn how I think. Ultimately, it boils down to how you think; what you believe you are capable of and what you feel you deserve. It's more important than the actual techniques. There are lots of ways to trade the market and there are lots of ways to get rich, but the most important thing is to believe in yourself.

You said "keep your ego in check," do you think humility is an important trait for a good trader?

There is a fine line between confidence and cockiness. But there's a saying that's been on Wall Street for a very long time: there are old traders and there are bold traders, but there aren't many old, bold traders. The market has a way of humbling traders with big egos. I'm a pretty confident guy, but when it comes to the market, I'm as humble as they come. The market is bigger than you'll ever be, so you have to take a back seat and that's really tough for people. They have a hard time being the caboose and letting the market be the engine.

Do you view yourself as a trader or an investor and what do you think the difference is?

My definition of an investor is someone who holds for long-term capital gains; one year or more rather than weeks or months. My longer-term trades tend to last two or three quarters, while my short-term trades could be days to weeks. It depends on the situation.

When I first started trading, I was more of an investor because back then commissions and spreads were huge; you couldn't move in and out quickly. It was much more cumbersome to place trades. So, you held stocks for bigger gains. When commissions came down, spreads narrowed and quick online access became available, that's when people started trading short term. I switched over to a shorter time-frame because I could compound my money faster and trade around positions. I would classify myself as a short to intermediate term swing trader.

Do you think your approach can successfully be copied?

I don't think it can be copied, I *know* it can! Many of our Minervini Private Access members and Master Trader Program workshop attendees are successfully executing my strategy every year here in the U.S. and also around the world. In fact, it probably works better in some foreign markets where there are many more inefficiently priced securities. Absolutely it can be duplicated.

Are you still trading as much as you used to?

I still trade every day, but I'm not as aggressive or as active as I was in the beginning of my career. Fortunately, I don't have to be. I'm older now and enjoy family life, hobbies and passing the torch to others. But I still love it and it's my passion. I also realized that I'm passionate about mentoring. It's a great feeling to see someone succeed and to know that you inspired them to dream and achieve.

We've had some volatility in the market recently. What is your reading of the market and how it's likely to perform over 2018?

I'm smart enough to know, that I'm not smart enough to predict very far out, so I would never bet on a prediction. The market is the engine and I'm just the caboose. I watch where the train goes and I follow along. But I'll tell you what to look out for, which could signify a major change in the market.

Until just recently we've had some of the lowest volatility we've ever seen and the market has been making very steady progress. That was happening because we have a moderate growth environment with very low inflation in the U.S. All around the world, the reigniting of growth hasn't really been strong enough to cause inflation, but world economies are growing.

Now if you look back prior to the 1980s, the boom and bust cycles were much wider. There were huge swings from deep recessions to big expansions. That volatility in the economic cycle led to volatility in stocks and the market went sideways for decades.

What's going to change will be whether we sink into a recession and the growth slows, or if inflation starts taking off and the economy gets too strong meaning that the Fed would have to jack rates more aggressively to engineer a recession. You have to look for a break-out in either direction from this stable moderate growth environment.

What do you do to control your risk in different market conditions - and do you change your strategy depending on whether the market is beginning to rise or fall?

I'm mainly watching the individual stocks. If there are stocks that meet my criteria then I buy them. If not, then I go to cash. If there are a lot of stocks that are showing short set-ups and there are no long set-ups, then I might entertain the short side. But I'm never just jumping in 100 percent right from cash. I use what I call progressive exposure, which just means testing the water with some pilot positions before you jump in with both feet.

So, maybe you go 25 percent invested, or even 50 percent invested, but you move in incrementally and you don't step it up until you've got some traction with those initial positions. If you're profitable, those profits can be used to finance additional risk or more aggressive positions and it'll cushion you a bit. You might miss a few weeks of market action before you're fully invested, but that's not going to make a big difference. The bottom line is: there's no sense in moving your exposure to 75 or 100 percent - or on margin - if you're not profitable at 25 percent or 50%, etc..

You won't get in too much trouble if you use progressive exposure and trade stock by stock as they emerge. I don't really need to look at anything but the stocks themselves. As a matter of fact, I would strongly encourage traders to take the indexes off their screens and try to operate just looking at stocks. I call it the Minervini "vacuum pack" challenge. See if you can go one year without looking at the indexes during the trading day. Most people can't go a few weeks or even a few days. But if you do, you will likely improve your results.

Do you consider whether a company has an attractive long-term future before making a trade?

That's a good question. One thing you have to remember about high growth stocks is that you can only see so far out with any degree of accuracy. Generally, that's only a few quarters. Even the best analysts are only going to be able to look forward a few quarters. Even the company's CEO has no idea for sure what will happen a year or two down the road. Business conditions could change, the economy can change and all types of things can happen - but that's the whole reason why there is opportunity. Not everything can be priced into a stock. If you could figure out what will happen a few years down the road, everything would be priced in. There would be no inefficient pricing and no opportunity.

That's why companies with huge growth - and you should always look for companies with huge growth potential - go higher and higher and defy gravity for years and years and can make huge multi-year moves. No analyst can put a correct multiple on a company growing earnings by 100 percent per quarter. And, there's no telling how long that will last. It could stop in three quarters or it could be a Cisco (NASDAQ:CSCO) and go for 16 quarters and the stock goes up 70,000 percent.

Take Amazon (NASDAQ:AMZN), which is now ruling the retail world. When I was buying Amazon in 1997, not only was there no visibility and no-one really understood their vision, Wall Street hated it. Analyst said Amazon (and some included the Internet as a whole) would never make money and it was the same for names like Yahoo and Microsoft (NASDAQ:MSFT). Believe it or not, these were relatively small cap names that few people knew. You want to go with the names that are smaller and unfamiliar to most people. That's where the real opportunity is.

So, how do you adjust to changing fundamentals?

You just have to go day by day, quarter by quarter, and as things change you change. Stick with the stock while it's reporting good earnings and the stock is acting right. Are the technicals confirming what's happening with the fundamentals? At some point those prospects are going to dim and you move on to something else.

With growth stocks all you need to look at are earnings, sales and margins - and the chart. Make sure the chart is agreeing with the fundamentals. Never bet on your fundamental ideas without confirmation from the technicals. You should ask, if things are so good but the stock isn't going up, why? There is almost always something going on you just don't know yet.

A number of Stockopedia members are using your methods in small cap stocks. Can your technique of buying on pullbacks after rising on high volume get good results in stocks of this size?

In the 1990s, I was an adviser to some of the big hedge funds, as well as some smaller hedge funds that were in faraway places like Chile and Peru. These were places where there might have been only 50 or 100 stocks on the entire stock exchange. But what I found was the opposite of what most people would imagine. While you have to have enough trading to have a market in a stock, the smaller the stock, the smaller it trades and the less it's followed, the more likely it is that it's inefficiently priced. Therefore, all other things being equal, it has greater potential for a bigger gain.

If you're trading Coca-Cola (NYSE:KO), which may be followed by 60 analysts, there is not much that can surprise. Plus, it's so large that it's very hard to move the stock. But if you've got some small company with five million shares in its float, and they suddenly they get a contract that will add a couple of dollars to their earnings, that can easily double the stock price. I love the smaller names that have smaller floats and trade lower volumes, as long it has a good chart and supporting fundamentals.

Do you find that you need to make adjustments to your rules - particularly with stop losses - when you are trading smaller companies?

It's actually the larger-cap names than tend to cause the most trouble. They whip around and give you more of the back and forth action that's likely to stop you out. The smaller names are the ones that will breakout and just go and get you a profit very quickly. So, it's just the opposite. It turns out to be counter-intuitive for people because big names are seen as safe. If you are using a very tight stop and the stock is a "crowded trade" (lots of retail eyes on it), you could get knocked out a bunch of times. I want a stock that really is flatlining because not many people follow it, and then it explodes and gets me a profit right away. I don't really have any kind of volume cut-off. If it's a smaller name, I just adjust my position size accordingly.

As far as the stop is concerned, I generally feel that if you can't be right within an 8 or 10 percent stop, you probably have bigger problems with your selection criteria or your entry technique, because 10 percent is a pretty big stop. During my entire career, my average loss is about four or five percent and that's with slippage and stocks gapping down on earnings included. Rarely do I take a large loss and I never adjust my stop for volatility. In both my books I explain how I attack volatility. My approach is just the opposite of what most do or what you might imagine.

Do you foresee a time when so many people are trying to trade your system that it stops working?

If there were hundreds of millions of people following me then maybe it could be a short-term risk. But I'm certainly not that popular. On top of that, it's not the cause it's the effect. Of all the people that are interested in what I'm doing, an even following me very closely, most don't have the discipline to do it. Even if you have a system you still have to stick to it.

William O'Neil got pretty popular, he had his own newspaper and wrote a book that sold over a million copies and even had a TV show for a while. But it never did anything to make his strategy ineffective.

But let's just say it did. Let's just say it got so popular that it made it ineffective. Guess what? Everybody would stop using it and then it would work great all over again!

Here's a perfect example... over the past few years, people have been saying that breakouts don't work anymore. When I heard "breakouts don't work!" - that was music to my ears, Last year, what happened? Breakouts worked perfectly. I've never seen so many stocks break out and hold their stops.

This is why you have to be committed to a strategy, because sometimes you have to go through periods when it doesn't work as well as it did before. Maybe you'll have a year when your style is out of vogue. If you stick with it, you'll be there for when it comes back in vogue. But if you switch and try to do different things, you'll never be good at any one thing, and it's unlikely you will switch back at the right time.

What I do is timeless, that why I spent 34 years perfecting it. It's a career, not a lottery ticket.

You've become really well known for the Master Trader Workshop that you hold every year. How is that event going?

We've been selling it out every year and we've had to think about whether to make it larger, but for now we cap it at around 100 people. I think last year we stretched it a bit and allowed 120. It has turned into an amazing, life-changing event for those who attend. I've never been so proud of a product I developed in my life. David Ryan and myself spend three days going over everything A-Z. On the third day, we trade live and I spend part of the day working with everyone on mindset and psychology. These traders come from all around the world - representing more than 50 countries, it's been incredible and the people I have met have all been really amazing!

Finally, if there was one thing that you'd like any individual to take from your books, what would it be?

Remember, records are made to be broken. Anything that somebody else does can not only be duplicated, but it can be exceeded because you have the benefit of starting where they left off. If you are fortunate to be able to do what you love, you should then teach it to others and pass the torch - and hope you inspire them to do it even better. That's what life is about.

The main thing to come away with is to believe in your own abilities. That's really the most important thing - you need to believe you can do it.

Otherwise, all the training in the world isn't going to make you hugely successful. And, I'm telling you with 100% certainty that you can!

I believe in people more than they believe in themselves, because I made it starting with nothing. I know every single person is only operating at a fraction of their potential.

You can only achieve what you believe. So, believe in yourself, commit to a process, be persistent and never give up and you will get to the top.

[Website Source https://seekingalpha.com/]

Common Mistakes That Beginners Make

Investing in the stock market can be exciting. It can also generate feelings of fear and despair. These emotional rollercoasters can lead new investors into making bad decisions. Many new investors also fail to educate themselves about how the markets work and the things they need to pay attention to. We all make mistakes, and these factors and more can lead to costly mistakes that lead to loss of capital. However, if you take some time to educate yourself and prepare ahead of time, you can minimize your mistakes and the costs of mistakes that you do make.

Prepare Before You Start Investing

Many people who decide they want to get into the stock market are anxious to do so. However, it's important to prepare before you start buying shares. The first thing that every person should do is make sure that they have an emergency fund of cash stashed away, and that you will not use it to buy stocks or to cover losses. The purpose of an emergency fund is to have money on hand in case you hit the skids with a job or lose other sources of income if you have a car or medical emergency, or your basement floods and you need to pay for expensive home repairs. Recent surveys have shown that far too many Americans have been neglecting basic savings, and many could not even meet a $400 emergency car repair. If you are in a situation where you couldn't pay for a $400 car repair, then you are not quite ready to get into the stock market. You should work to save up a little bit of money first. Many experts recommend that you save up around six months of required funds to pay all your living expenses, and that is good advice, however that doesn't mean you have to wait that long to start investing, but you should at least get two months ahead before you start buying stocks.

Another important part of preparation is education. And congratulations, by reading this, you've demonstrated that you are the kind of person who is willing to take time to learn before jumping into something! That is a very important consideration, especially when money is involved. You should also look into courses that are available online and read as many books as possible, especially when trying to determine what kind of risks you are willing to take and how to marry your investment goals with that. There are many online courses available on basic stock investing, day trading, swing trading, options, and other topics. There are even many good videos you can watch on YouTube to get a grasp of many of the basic topics.

In recent years the development of simulators is one of the most exciting tools for education. These can be really useful, especially if you've never done self-directed investing before, but especially for those who are looking to be day traders, swing traders, or trade options. Practice makes perfect as they say, and that's as true with investing and trading as it is with anything else. If it's important for a football player to practice before a game, it's important for a new trader to practice day trading or options trading, before putting real money on the line.

- Investing or Trading Based on Emotions Rather Than Facts

One problem with investing and trading are that emotions ride high. It's completely natural to experience emotional highs and lows as the stock market does its usual roller coaster ride. However, what you don't want to do is let emotions start guiding your decisions and taking you over.

The process of being guided by emotion can start at the very beginning when you choose your very first stock to invest in. Ask yourself a question – why are you choosing that particular company? Are you picking different companies because you think they are cool, or because you are really taking a cold hard look at company fundamentals? You should be selecting companies based on whether or not they meet your investment goals. So you should be looking at their earnings, their future prospects, the P/E ratio and other important metrics that will help you decide whether or not a company is 1) in good shape both now and for the long term future as far as you can see it, and 2) that the company actually helps you meet your investment goals.

Maybe you are in love with Apple. But being in love with Apple is not a good enough reason to buy stock in Apple. If Apple doesn't match up with your investment goals, you should be looking elsewhere.

Emotion has a huge influence when people are facing losses. People panic and sell off. When the Dow Jones starts declining, people start moving their cash into "safe" investments, many that these days don't even pay hardly anything like money market funds. Some people don't even do that and just sell out and take the cash.

As an investor, you need to be disciplined. The courses of action described in the last paragraph that is governed by fear and panic are not the courses of action that a disciplined investor is going to take. Now if you are a swing trader and the market is declining, then either you're going to sell, or you're going to be shorting the stock. If you are a long-time investor, however, you most certainly shouldn't follow the lemmings over the cliff. What you should be doing is looking at a downturn as a buying opportunity. So, you should be loading up on shares, but don't do it all at once. When the market enters a downturn, nobody can be sure how low it's going to go, so you want to make disciplined, periodic purchases the way you always do. Dollar cost averaging always works when you are in it for the long haul. That doesn't mean you won't miss some opportunities, but over time the market will rebound again, and by the time you are in your retirement years, the prices will be much higher than they were when you originally invested in most cases.

There are going to be some cases when you're going to want to bail. An individual stock can decline for many reasons, and sometimes there is a point of no return. For example, Bear Sterns crashed from $170 a share to $2 a share over a matter of a few weeks. If you had invested in Bear Sterns, then you should have been studying the situation closely and you would have gotten out early.

So, you might want to bail from an individual stock when the data tells you that this is the right course of action. But you never get out of any stock simply based on panic. Know what the fundamentals are of the company.

Emotion works the other way too. When it seems like a stock simply goes up and up, people can start getting giddy about it. You might be tempted to put your entire life savings into that one stock. But that is a bad idea, no matter how good the stock is. As we've mentioned before, it's great to know that Amazon increased so much that an investment of a few thousand would have made you a millionaire, but hindsight is 20/20. Right now, it's impossible to know which if any social media companies are going to actually bank profits and still be around in 20 years, so it would be foolish to put your life savings into one. The so-called investor who goes around claiming to know what the next sure thing is can be called nothing more than a fool.

Another problem is people get emotionally invested in one company. Maybe it's because of the mission of the company or the products it makes that people think are going to "change the world." But when you get emotionally invested in a company, you start becoming irrational. Good examples include Tesla and Theranos. Let's take the latter case. Theranos claimed to have invented a revolutionary means to let people test their blood and to have medications delivered. It became clear that it was a sham, but the people who were emotionally invested in the company and the female CEO were literally fooled about it – and some still are even though it's clear now that Theranos is done and the CEO may even be facing charges.

In the case of Tesla, the jury is still out. They make high-quality products but have problems with delivery and scaling. They may yet overcome those problems. But if you talk to many Tesla investors, they are zealots about it. If Tesla ends up going down the drain, many of the investors may go down with it. Is it worth it?

To avoid letting emotion take over whether you get swept up with the lemmings running off the cliff when there is a bear market, whether you panic when an individual stock starts dropping, or whether you get hyper-excited when your favorite company is booming, you need to have rules in place beforehand and follow them.

For example, one rule that you could have in place is you never invest more than 5% of your portfolio in any single company. If you do that, then you are not going to be damaged even if you're a bit taken in by the company or you panic when it drops – or worse – miss when you should get out. Think about the poor fools who stayed invested in Bear Sterns until the end, and even the government wouldn't bail them out.

This is one reason why I like ETFs, although you don't have to use them for your entire portfolio. They divorce you from the problems that can arise when you start getting emotionally invested in one stock.

- Putting Too Much Stake in the past Performance

One mistake many new (and even experienced) investors make is putting too much credence in the past performance of a stock. The fact is, as they say in the disclaimer, past performance is not a guarantee of future returns.

So, people often look at past performance as a guarantee of future performance when history shows that it is more often than not, simply not true. So, you might've seen a run-up of some particular stock over the last year, maybe it was Netflix, or maybe it was Amazon. And so, you just expected to continue. Of course, the real world doesn't work that way and the expected returns may not materialize. As it is, although none of us can tell the future, the run-ups of Netflix and Amazon may have come to an end. Of course, over the very long term, we probably expect both of those to grow. We simply don't know, so putting all of your investments into Netflix isn't a good idea, but you might want to put some of your investments into Netflix.

So, let's take Apple as another example. Apple has had an incredible run up over the past 10 to 12 years. Ever since they introduced the first iPhone, growth has been spectacular, expectations have been high, and returns have been even better. We really haven't seen anything quite like it before.

Apple is still a solid company, but one thing you can say is that it has run into a stall. Right now, nobody is expecting Apple to make the huge leaps that it did for the past 12 years. You could've invested in Apple in 2014 say and simply expected the run-ups to continue. What you couldn't foresee is that Apple was running out of new inventions already back then. Without Steve Jobs at the helm, it's hard to see Apple rebounding and getting back to the spectacular growth experience that they had before. Of course, you never know, maybe they will bring in some new management that has some of the talents that Jobs did, and they will recover their lead. But before you invest, you should be tracking what the company is doing.

So, I hate to beat a dead horse, but this is one that needs to be beaten. I spent a lot of time talking about index funds, but a lot of times that advice will fall on deaf ears. People that want to have a self-directed investment fund find them boring.

Here are the facts. There are some investors that have a fantastic ability to pick individual stocks that are going to be winners. And it's fun doing it. I don't want to discourage you from picking your own individual stocks. But like I also said I tend to put 50% of my investments in exchange-traded funds. The reality is that most people don't have all the time in the world to be studying companies, market trends, and the like in order to pick good stocks.

Now if you do follow my advice and limit yourself to picking maybe 10 stocks, then you're on the way toward more success. At least, under those circumstances, you don't have to spend 24 hours a day studying companies in the markets. However, broad index funds that give you approximately the same returns as the total Stock market, so they are a fantastic way to invest and build long term wealth. The answer is to follow both paths even if you use a different asset allocation than I have.

- Diversifying, but Not Really Diversifying

So, you build your investment portfolio. And you come and tell me that you've decided to go with picking all individual stocks. And then you tell me that you've invested in 25 companies. Sounds fantastic! But then you tell me they're all banks.

Remember that when you diversify, that doesn't just mean picking different companies. It also means diversifying across sectors, company size, and even investing in different types of securities like bonds. You might even consider investing in different overseas markets, including Europe, Japan, China, and developing countries. Diversifying helps you weather storms that don't impact the entire economy but might hit one sector hard. At the time of writing, because of trade disputes, you might be in a world of hurt if you invested in soybeans, while the rest of the economy is humming along. Diversification is so important it should be mentioned often.

Conclusion

Thank for making it through to the end of this, let's hope it was informative and able to provide you with all of the tools you need to achieve your goals whatever they may be.

The next step is to start practicing your stock trading skills, stock markets analysis, applying different strategies, and how to use the various financial tools including chart reading. All these are pretty simple and straightforward. If you put your heart and mind to it, then you will get to eventually learn and understand how the stock markets function.

It is amazing to learn that buying and selling stocks is a pretty simple affair. Most traders and investors, including novices, are able to pull this off. The main challenge will be to learn how to choose the winners. There are quite a number of stocks in all the different industries and sectors of the economy. If you learn how to identify the winning stocks, then you can expect your investments to grow immensely over the years.

A lot of investors across America and elsewhere around the world have managed to create wealth for themselves and their families through stock market investments. You too can achieve this success through prudent investments over time. There are different strategies and approaches to stock market investing. If you can find the right approach and be committed to the strategy you choose, then you will enjoy long term success. Remember to start investing as soon as possible because the sooner you start the better off you will be.